The Puerto Rican Poets

•

Los Poetas Puertorriqueños

•

Edited by
Alfredo Matilla
and
Iván Silén

A NATIONAL GENERAL COMPANY

To Hugo
A.M.
I.S.

RL1: VLM 8 (VLR 6-8) / IL 10-up

THE PUERTO RICAN POETS
A Bantam Book / published August 1972

COPYRIGHT NOTICES AND ACKNOWLEDGMENTS

Library of Congress Cataloging in Publication Data

Matilla, Alfredo, comp.
The Puerto Rican poets.

Poems in Spanish with English translation.
1. Puerto Rican poetry (Collections) I. Silén, Iván, joint comp.
II. Title. III. Title: Los poetas puertorriqueños.
PQ7434.M35 861'.008 72-3959

Published simultaneously in the United States and Canada

Bantam Books are published by Bantam Books, Inc., a National General company. Its trade-mark, consisting of the words "Bantam Books" and the portrayal of a bantam is registered in the United States Patent Office and in other countries. Marca Registrada. Bantam Books, Inc., 666 Fifth Avenue, New York, N.Y. 10019.

PRINTED IN THE UNITED STATES OF AMERICA

Contents

Part Two: The Major Poets

Part Three: Latest Poetry (from 1955)

Prologue

The purpose of this anthology is to bring together most of the important Puerto Rican poetry of this century for both Spanish- and English-speaking readers. To our knowledge, it is the first book to cover the entire range of Puerto Rican poetry from Luis Llorens Torres to Hugo Margenat, from Evaristo Ribera Chevremont to Pedro Pietri. It is also the first book to include both the works of writers who have developed revolutionary concepts of language and reality and the works of more "pure" writers dating from before 1955. It is also the first volume to include poems that express the full range of the Puerto Rican's experience in New York—their anger, their will for struggle, their vision of their particular world, their sense of themselves as victims of a universal process of displacement, driven from their homeland to a strange metropolis. In putting together the book, we have gone back over the entire history of contemporary Puerto Rican poetry, basing our selections on our idea of what constitutes a *major poet* and also upon a radical criterion of what is and what ought to be the craft of the poet.

Poets Before 1955

Part I includes the works of those writers who have had an impact either technically or creatively on the poetry in Puerto Rico before 1955. At about this time Hugo Margenat wrote his major work and he is the bridge between the older and the younger generation.

The "Trauma" and Modernism

After the North American invasion in 1898, artistic creation in Puerto Rico ceased for several years. In response to the new political situation of the island created by the move from Spanish colonial control to North American control, a more politically oriented literature developed that was better able to explain and interpret what had happened.

During this period, Latin-American modernism arrived in Puerto Rico. As a movement, it was one of the first affirmations of the distinctiveness of the Americas. It was a significant influence in Puerto Rico around 1912, primarily through the *Revista de las Antillas*, and continued to be more or less dominant until about 1925, when Puerto Rican poets began to create their own schools.

Modernism affirmed the Indian element common to all the American cultures, but it generally excluded the influence of black cultures in Puerto Rico. Modernism was American toward Europe and Hispanic toward the United States. It had an immediate impact because it created a new style that was antagonistic to the cultural penetration of the United States. It reaffirmed the Puerto Rican national culture in the face of North American cultural, economic, and political imperialism.

Luis Llorens Torres passed from the modernist avant-garde orientation of the *Revista de las Antillas* to a more localist frame of reference. He struggled to find the roots of what is distinctively Puerto Rican. But as a poet, he gives the sense more of a general returning home from his last defeat than an artist moving toward the future. His political position is based on nostalgia for Spain, the mother country. At bottom, his work reflects his own high creole bourgeoisie vision of the world, a perspective that is his not only by birth but by vocation. Unlike the verses of Julia de Burgos, his work never extends beyond the limits of the "propriety" of his social class.

Another of the important modernists is Evaristo Ribera Chevremont (b. 1896). Like all writers who are unable to make a definitive break with the modernist idea, his work is diluted. He remains behind his reality and, by extension, ours. He sings a song without roots in the soil even in his last, more avant-garde works where he attains his greatest successes. His fusion of the "classic" and the "pure" has given his poetry a recognition among critics from Spain that is very rare in the history of Puerto Rican poetry.

Militance

After Pachín Marín, Juan Antonio Corretjer (b. 1908) is the first poet to embody a revolutionary ambition in his work. And it is because of this that many critics have tried to ignore him. Regardless, his influence passes on through Hugo Margenat to subsequent generations. Corretjer sees in the indigenous, the roots that mold us as a nation. His poetry is almost always infused with a deep-rooted lyricism. The persecution of Corretjer continues until the present.

The work of Francisco Matos Paoli (b. 1915) involves a struggle to liberate himself from his obsessive idea of God.

The shock of incarceration (he was brutally treated in prison as a result of his separatist ideas) manifests itself in alienating violence. He seems to have used the idea of God to mitigate his experience of the prisons La Princesa and Oso Blanco. Unfortunately, even his greatest work, *Canto de la locura* (1962), with its illuminating portrait of chaos, written with nails and blood on the walls of the cell, dissolves in a watered-down concept of divinity. In 1969 he published *El viento y la paloma,* in which religion, which has pursued him since infancy, snatches him away from insanity, although it doesn't necessarily elevate him as a poet. His last verses (*La marea sube,* 1971) are structured from a clear and bold position against North American neocolonialism and a fresh approach to the language of daily things. They bring him closer to the pure expression of his hidden feelings.

Major Poets

Part II groups three major poets, most of whose work was completed before 1960, Luis Palés Matos, Julia de Burgos, and Hugo Margenat. In the terms of this anthology, a *major poet* is one who, in a given historical moment, is able to re-embody in his inner self the reality in which he lives. His vision of the world is a summary of the vital trends of his people and his generation: he is both an echo and a new voice. He has shed the bourgeois values and morality of his society in order to seek out meteoric sparks. He combines a dedication to the word of his people with a commitment to his history. When a *major poet* speaks of himself, he also expresses his deepest thoughts about his people, his country, and of man. Thus, in him, there is neither folklore nor alienation. His metaphoric language is new because it joins two almost irreconcilable extremes in a repressive society: the individual and the "collective unconsciousness."

Luis Palés Matos (1898–1959) is our great poet who first discovered our "innermost being" after the "trauma" of the American invasion of 1898. To appreciates Palés, one must understand where he was born: Guayama (black world); bourgeoisie (white world of the landowners). He begins from this double foundation and culminates in *Tuntun de pasa y grifería,* one of the first Caribbean poetic interpretations of the black experience. His "white" works never really reach a synthesis of his double self, in spite of the fact that in various poems the union of the white and the black seem to arrive at a resolution. (At times, he is guilty of racist attitudes and vocabulary which are a product of his social class and the prejudice of a period that conceived of the African as sex, jungle, drums, and dance. The great merit of Palés is that, almost against the grain, he has dealt with the black and the Hispanic—or European—as a fundamental basis of the Puerto Rican-Antillean—Matilla.*)

Palés may also be the first to create the myth of our gestalt by uncovering the Antillean subconscious. Palés grows by affirming the contradiction of his environment. It is neither Mother Goose nor Little Red Riding Hood nor the Wolf who has adorned his childhood fantasy but rather the stories of the black mammy. (In this sense we can say that when Palés deals with his Caribbean heritage, he responds to it unconsciously as a man rooted in what is black. When he makes fun of the black, he doesn't laugh at our spinal column, but at a hispanicizing colonial heritage that comes to the black man when he forgets himself and wants to become white. In his other poetry, Palés appears to be tormented by the seeming hopelessness of the Puerto Rican independence movement and by academic nihilism—Silén.*) In his later poetry, he finds himself and begins a song so new that even his own critics have not been able to decipher it.

When Julia de Burgos (1914–1953) comes to us in *Poema en veinte surcos* she is already both lyrical and rebellious. Her poetry is so agonizing that each verse seems like an act of suicide. "Give me my number, because if not, I will die after I'm dead!" Afterwards, she will continue erupting in different voices, surprising those of us who still remember her *Canción de la verdad sencilla.*

In her life the social injustice of her time repeats itself on a personal as well as a political level, as in Corretjer and Matos Paoli. She was ignored by critics, silenced by institutes, and cast aside by localist poets who drove her to an alcoholic explosion that frightened the Puerto Rican bourgeoisie. Her poetry is a continuous attempt to maintain a balance in her existence, to yoke together the individual problem of her existence with that of justice and country.

Into the introspective desert of the poets of the 50s Hugo Margenat (1933–1957) appeared. The three great themes of Puerto Rican poetry, God, love, and country, radiate from his poetry. *Mundo abierto* (posthumous, 1958) picks up the political militancy that was closed to Corretjer and Matos Paoli,

---

* Passages where the two editors have disagreed or had separate opinions are indicated by their names.

without ever converting his poetry into propaganda pamphlets. He shows us a living historical reality. For him, God is metaphysics, everyday truth, conspirator, obsession, a glass of beer, political thought, comrade:

> Leftist God
> is the perpetual conspirator

and later:

> I and God have returned to you. With wooden wings.

His treatment of love portrays feelings of anxiety, of closed space:

> She, her face turned to organic decay
> doesn't return, doesn't return

He parallels Julia de Burgos with his sense of the timeless desperation of lost love. Hugo:

> Oh, if I had you. I have had you.

and Julia:

> Only to sing to you awakens me.

They continue a parallel descent toward death; Hugo:

> I am the multitude
> of sandals
> walking.

Julia:

> It must be the useless caress,
> the endless sadness of being a poet,
> of singing and singing, without breaking
> the unparalleled tragedy of existence.

As with Julia de Burgos, love leads him to death.

The themes of Margenat, which originate in previous poetry and are assimilated toward the future, pass to the young poets of the generation of the 70s who take them as a battle flag in its three aspects.

Latest Poetry

Part III includes those poets who have written since Hugo Margenat. We have tried to select the most representative work of the young poets without attempting any definitive judgment. We are too closely immersed in that poetic universe. If we have omitted any writer in this anthology, it hasn't been out of carelessness.*

The new poetry on the whole is an experience in crisis. The modern poet arises, undone, traumatized, to split the word (broken in that very instant and even before by a colonized society, in Puerto Rico, as well as in the ghettos of New York), to resist the foreign invasion, be it hispanicizing or saxonizing (moving toward a parallel with Latin America, with the countries of the Third World), to rediscover the collective face, to give testimony to a rending of past and present (the Spanish colonies and the North American) that rush headlong toward a new day (liberation). Poetry of urgency, of the street (mostly that of New York). The poets become brothers crossing a bridge of airplanes that span language. The oppressive existence is manifest from the same assumptions: exploitation, colonization, racism, occupation. Brothers in the poetic task that for us is struggle—the fundamental political position (the defeat of imperialism) and in the fact that the liberation of the Puerto Rican must be achieved on the island as well as the United States, where a third of our people are agonizing.

There are two tendencies in the new poetry: one which is born from a kind of obstinate nationalism that leads to socialist realism, and the other, that of the poets who explore their revolutionary commitment from myth and hallucination.

Puerto Rican poetry of the twentieth century, in Puerto Rico as well as New York, with a few exceptions, is a struggle against the agony of the ghetto (in the colony and the metropolis) and against the imposition of a crushing colonial state of mind. It is a battle against the occupation of our soil and our culture by the United States. It is a summons to awaken from this broken English dream and assume the Puerto Rican and Latin-American essence that belongs to us.

ALFREDO MATILLA
IVÁN SILÉN

2 June 1971, New York City

---

* The group of Guajana, which refused to cooperate with us on this *Anthology*.

Part One

MOST IMPORTANT POETS BEFORE 1955

Luis Llorens Torres (1876–1944)

El patito feo

No sé si danés o ruso,
genial cuentista relata
que en el nido de una pata
la hembra de un cisne puso.
Y ahorrando las frases de uso
en los cuentos eruditos,
diz que sin más requisitos,
en el tricésimo día,
la pata sacó su cría
de diez y nueve patitos.

Según este cuento breve,
creció el rebaño pigmeo
llamando PATITO FEO
al patito diez y nueve.
¡El pobre! Siempre la nieve
lo encontró fuera del ala.
Y siempre erró en la antesala
de sus diez y ocho hermanos
que dejábanle sin granos
las espigas de la tala.

Vagando por la campaña
la palmípeda cuadrilla
al fin llegó hasta la orilla
de la fuente en la montaña.
¡Qué sensación tan extraña
y a la par tan complaciente
la que le onduló en la mente
al llamado FEO PATO
cuando miró su retrato
en el vidrio de la fuente!

The Ugly Duckling

Don't know if Danish or Russian,
a genius of a storyteller narrates
that in a duck's nest
a female swan lay.
And setting aside the phrases used
in learned stories,
let's say without further ado,
that on the fortnight,
the duck brought forth her brood
of nineteen ducklings.

According to this short tale,
the pygmy herd grew
calling the nineteenth one
the Ugly Duckling.
Poor thing! Always the snow
caught him outside the wing.
And he always erred in the anteroom
of his eighteen brothers
who, without grains, left him
the thorns in the garden patch.

Roaming through the countryside
the web-footed troop
finally reached the edge
of the fountain in the mountain.
What a strange but
altogether pleasing sensation
rippled through the mind
of the so-called Ugly Duckling
when he saw his image
in the glass of the fountain!

Surgió entonces de la umbría
un collar de cisnes blancos
en cuyos sedosos flancos
la espuma se emblanquecía.
(Aquí, al autor, que dormía
cuando este cuento soñó,
dicen que lo despertó
la emoción de la belleza.
Y aquí sigue, o aquí empieza,
lo que tras él soñé yo.)

Cisne azul la raza hispana
puso un huevo, ciega y sorda,
en el nido de la gorda
pata norteamericana.
Y ya, desde mi ventana,
los norteños patos veo,
de hosco pico fariseo,
que al cisne de Puerto Rico,
de azul pluma y rojo pico,
le llaman PATITO FEO.

Pueblo que cisne naciste,
mira y sonríe, ante el mote,
con sonrisa del Quijote
y con su mirada triste;
que a la luz del sol que viste
de alba tu campo y tu mar,
cuando quieras contemplar
que es de cisne tu figura,
mírate en al agua pura
de la fuente de tu hogar.

Con flama de tu real sello,
mi cisne de Puerto Rico,
la lumbre roja del pico
prendes izada en el bello
candelabro de tu cuello.
Y azul del celeste tul,
en que une la Cruz del Sur

Then from the shade sprung
a chain of white swans
on whose silky sides
the foam became white.
(Here, the author, who was sleeping
when he dreamed this story,
they say he was awakened
by the emotion of such beauty.
And here continues, or here begins,
what after him I dreamed.)

Blue swan the Hispanic race
lay an egg, blind and deaf,
in the nest of the fat
North American duck.
And already, from my window,
I see the northern ducks,
of gloomy, hypocritical peak,
who the swan of Puerto Rico,
of blue plumage and red peak,
they called the Ugly Duckling.

Nation born swan
looks and smiles, before the mockery
with a Quixote smile
and a sad look;
the sunlight dresses as dawn
your countryside and sea
when you want to see
your figure of a swan,
look at yourself in the pure water
of your home's fountain.

With the flame of your regal seal,
my swan of Puerto Rico,
the red fire of your peak
lights up hoisted on the beautiful
candelabra of your neck.
And the blue of celestial tulle,
where the Cross of the South

sus cinco brillantes galas,
es el que pinta en tus alas
tu firme triángulo azul.

Oro latino se asoma
a tu faz y en tu faz brilla.
Lo fundió en siglos Castilla.
Y antes de Castilla, Roma.
Lo hirvió el pueblo de Mahoma
en sus fraguas sarracenas.
Y antes de Roma, en Atenas,
los Homero y los Esquilo
hilaron de ensueño el hilo
de la hebra azul de tus venas.

En tu historia y religión
tus claros timbres están;
que fuiste el más alto afán
de Juan Ponce de León.
Mírate, con corazón,
en tu origen caballero,
en tu hablar latinoibero,
en la fe de tus altares,
y en la sangre audaz que en Lares
regó Manolo el Leñero.

Veinte cisnes como tú
nacieron contigo hermanos
en los virreinos hermanos
de Méjico y el Perú.
Bajo el cielo de tisú
de la antillana región,
los tres cisnes de Colón,
las tres cluecas carabelas,
fueron las aves abuelas
en tan magna incubación.

Alma de la patria mía,
cisne azul puertorriqueño,
si quieres vivir el sueño

unites its five brilliant graces,
paints your firm blue
triangle on your wings.

Latin gold looks out
from your face and shines in your face.
Was founded for centuries by Castile.
And before Castile, Rome.
Was brought to a boil by the people of Muhammad
in its moorish forges.
And before Rome, in Athens
the Homers and Aeschylus
spun the dream of
the blue thread of your veins.

In your history and religion
are your clear stampings:
that you were the biggest anxiety
of Juan Ponce de León.
Look at yourself, with heart
in your gentlemanly origin,
in your Latin-Iberic talk,
in the faith of your altars,
and in the fearless blood that in Lares
Manolo el Leñero shed.

Twenty swans like you
were born with you brothers
in the viceroyships brothers
of Mexico and Peru.
Beneath the golden sky
of the Antillian region,
Columbus' three swans
the three brooding caravels,
the birds were the grandmothers
in such a grand hatching.

Soul of my country,
blue Puerto Rican swan,
if you want to live the dream

de tu honor y tu hidalguía,
escucha la voz bravía
de tu independencia santa
cuando al cielo la levanta
el huracán del Caribe
que con sus rayos la escribe
y con sus truenos la canta.

Ya surgieron de la espuma
los veinte cisnes azules
en cuyos picos de gules
se desleirá la bruma.
A ellos su plumaje suma
el cisne de mi relato.
Porque ha visto su retrato
en los veinte cisnes bellos.
Porque quiere estar con ellos.
Porque no quiere ser pato.

El güiro en a-e-i-o-u

Trova jíbara de baile de Añonuevo
con güiro, guitarra y cuatro.

Chúscu-chúscu-chuchúscu-chúscu,
y de repente: ¡chus-chus-chús! . . .
Ya están adentro las parejas
en el baile de Don Chuchú.
Ahora bríndanle a la parranda
de Capitanejo y Arús:
por el Añonuevo, los Reyes,
La Virgen y el Niño Jesús.
Arroz con dulce y agualoja
y ron de caña Santa Cruz.
Don Chuchú, zumbándose un palo,
suelta un bostezo de anamú.

of your honor and nobility,
listen to the fearless voice
of your holy independence
when to heaven it's lifted
by the Caribbean hurricane
that writes with its lightning flashes
and sings with its thunders.

From the foam already sprung
the twenty blue swans
in whose red peaks
the mist will be diluted.
To them the swan of my tale
adds his plumage.
Because he saw his image
in the twenty beautiful swans.
Because he wants to be with them.
Because he doesn't want to be a duck.

(Translated by Digna Sánchez-Méndez)

The Güiro in A-E-I-O-U

Jíbaro dance for New Year's played on *güiro*, guitar, and *cuatro*.

Chúscu-chúscu-cuchúscu-chúscu,
and suddenly: chus-chus-chús! . . .
Already the couples are inside
at the dance of Don Chuchú.
Now an offering to the group
of Capitanejo and Arús:
for New Year's, Three Kings' Day,
the Virgin and Christ Child.
Arroz con dulce and *agualoja*
and San Cruz moonshine rum.
Don Chuchú, gulping a shot,
lets go a yawn of anamú.

El güiro ráscase y aúlla
bajando el risco de la u . . .
Chúscu-chúscu-cuchúscu-chúscu,
y de repente: ¡chus-chus-chús!

Chósco-cochósco-chósco-chósco,
y de repente: ¡chos-chos-chós! . . .
Están bailando el pavo-pavo.
Se enronquece el güiro en la o . . .
El pavo es Don Chuchú y le canta
esta bomba a María Laó.
Tu mamá te parió doncella,
ay léilo-léilo-loleiló,
pero en seguida te perdiste,
por no saber decir que no . . .
Chósco-cochósco-chósco-chósco,
y de repente: ¡chos-chos-chós! . . .

Chísqui-chísqui-quichísqui-chísqui,
y de repente: ¡chis-chis-chís! . . .
En la rumba, que va que zumba,
es el güiro el que da la i . . . ,
cuando Rita, que está que pita,
brincando atrás dice que sí,
y silba el coco de sus dientes,
y arde en sus labios el ají . . .
Chísqui-chísqui-quichísqui-chísqui,
y de repente: ¡chis-chis-chís! . . .

Chásca-chásca-chásca-cachásca,
y de repente: ¡chas-chas-chás! . . .
Es que entre el cuatro y la guitarra
el güiro está que viene y va;
aquí da un grito de alegría
y un ayayay de llanto allá;
mientras el jíbaro y la jíbara
se pegan más y más y más,
cara y cara, cara con cara,
boca y boca en mariyandá,
al loleiló-loléilo-leiló,

The *güiro* scratched and hooted
going down the cliff of the u . . .
Chúscu-chúscu-cuchúscu-chúscu,
and suddenly: chus-chus-chús!

Chósco-cochósco-chósco-chósco,
and suddenly: chos-chos-chós! . . .
They are dancing the *pavo-pavo.*
The *güiro* becomes hoarse on the o . . .
The *pavo* is Don Chuchú and he sings
this *bomba* to María Laó:
Your mother bore you maiden
ay léilo-léilo-loleiló,
but you quickly got lost
because of not knowing how to say no . . .
Chósco-cochósco-chósco-chósco,
and suddenly: chos-chos-chós! . . .

Chísqui-chísqui-quichísqui-chísqui,
and suddenly: chis-chis-chís! . . .
In the rumba, that goes buzzing,
it's the *güiro* that gives the i. . . ,
When Rita, who is hot,
running back says yes,
and whistles the coconut of her teeth,
and makes spices hot on her lips . . .
Chísqui-chísqui-quichísqui-chísqui,
and suddenly: chis-chis-chís! . . .

Chásca-chásca-chásca-cachásca,
and suddenly: chas-chas-chás! . . .
It's that between the guitar and the *cuatro*
the *güiro* swings in and out;
over here gives a yell of happiness
and over there an outcry of ayayay
while the *jíbaros*
get much, much, much closer,
face to face, face with face,
mouth to mouth *mariyandá,*
to the loleiló-loléilo-leiló,

pa' ti na' más, pa' ti na' más,
ay loleiló-léilo-loléilo,
repicando el güiro en la a . . .
Chásca-chásca-chásca-cachásca,
y de repente: ¡chas-chas-chás! . . .

Chésque-quechésque-chésque-chésque,
y de repente: ¡ches-ches-chés! . . .
Una maraca macaraca
dice que qué, que qué, que qué,
y el güiro güicharachero
quiere que quiere sin querer.
Relincha el güiro sobre ella:
¡jéje-jéjeje-jejejé! . . .
Vuelan los bancos y las sillas
y hecho pedazos el quinqué . . .
Dicen que el güiro y que se va . . .
Dicen que el güiro y que se fue . . .
Y en lo oscuro: chésque-quechésque,
corriendo el güiro tras la e . . . ,
Chésque-quechésque-chésque-chésque,
y de repente: ¡ches-ches-chés! . . .

for you only, for you only,
ay loleiló-léilo-loléilo,
the *güiro* peels in the a . . .
Chásca-chásca-chásca-cachásca,
and suddenly: chas-chas-chás! . . .

Chésque-quechésque-chésque-chésque,
and suddenly: ches-ches-chés! . . .
Ah, maraca *macaraca*
says and what, and what, and what,
and the *güiro güicharachero*
wants because wants without wanting.
The *güiro* neighs over her:
jéje-jéjeje-jejejé! . . .
The benches and seats flying
the lamp made pieces . . .
They say the *güiro* is leaving. . . .
They say that the *güiro* left. . . .
And in the darkness: chésque-quechésque,
the *güiro* running after the e. . . ,
Chésque-quechésque-chésque-chesqué,
and suddenly: ches-ches-chés! . . .

(Translated by Digna Sánchez-Méndez)

Evaristo Ribera Chevremont (b. 1896)

La sinfonía de los martillos

En el silencio áspero retumban los martillos.
Es una nueva música de vigoroso ritmo.
Es música que expone, con masculino empuje,
la rígida grandeza del proletario espíritu.

En el silencio áspero retumban los martillos.

Oyendo las canciones eróticas y burdas,
de tono desmayado, se cansan los oídos.
El hombre de hoy reclama la brusca sinfonía
forjada por la mano brutal de nuestro siglo.

En el silencio áspero retumban los martillos.

Retumban en talleres de llama y humareda.
Retumban, anchurosos, potentes, los martillos.
Y, al retumbar, descubren el alma del acero.
El alma del acero se entrega en el sonido.

En el silencio áspero retumban los martillos.

Retumban los martillos, retumban los martillos.
Retumban, anchurosos, potentes, los martillos.
Y apagan las dulzuras del piano y de la viola,
sutiles instrumentos de enervador fluído.

En el silencio áspero retumban los martillos.

Gavotas, minuetos, romanzas y oberturas
denuncian una época de magistral estilo;
pero la sinfonía de los martillos dice
de la pujanza cruda de un tiempo vasto en ímpetus.

Symphony of the Hammers

In the rough silence the hammers rumble.
A new music of vigorous cadence.
Music that with masculine strength reveals
the rigid grandeur of the proletarian spirit.

In the rough silence the hammers rumble.

The ears tire of listening to the faint sounds
of the coarse erotic songs.
The man of today demands the brusque symphony
forged by the brutal hand of our century.

In the rough silence the hammers rumble.

They rumble in factories of flame and smoke.
Vast and potent the hammers rumble.
And, rumbling, they discover the soul of steel.
The soul of steel surrenders in the sound.

In the rough silence the hammers rumble.

The hammers rumble, the hammers rumble.
Vast and potent the hammers rumble.
And they muffle the sweetness of the piano and the viola,
subtle instruments of weakened fluid.

In the rough silence the hammers rumble.

Gavottes, minuets, romanzas and overtures
denounce an epoch of masterful style
but the symphony of the hammers tells
of the crude power of a time vast in impetus.

En el silencio áspero retumban los martillos.

No es hora del perfume, ni es hora de las citas.
No es hora del deleite, ni es hora de los vinos.
No es hora del poema de untuosos maquillajes.
Es hora del poema del músculo y del grito.

En el silencio áspero retumban los martillos.

Retumban los martillos, retumban los martillos,
Retumban, anchurosos, potentes, los martillos.
Retumban los martillos. Su ruda sinfonía
me enseña la energía compacta de lo físico.

En el silencio áspero retumban los martillos.

En el silencio áspero retumban los martillos.
Es una nueva música de vigoroso ritmo.
Es música que expone, con masculino empuje,
la rígida grandeza del proletario espíritu.

En el silencio áspero retumban los martillos.

Cristo rojo

Más allá de las torres
animadas del vuelo de los pájaros,
hay una cruz, y en la cruz hay clavado un hombre.
Eres tú, Cristo rojo.
No es en el castillo, blando de alfombras, donde naces,
Cristo rojo.
Ni es el señor del cigarrillo de marfil y de ámbar el que te
engendra.
Te engendra la masa,
la masa espumante de Cristos,
la masa de sudor, de llanto y de sangre,

In the rough silence the hammers rumble.

It is not the hour of the perfume nor the hour of dates.
It is not the hour of pleasure, nor the hour of wines.
It is not the hour of greasy makeup.
It is the hour of the poem of the muscle and the scream.

In the rough silence the hammers rumble.

The hammers rumble, the hammers rumble.
Vast and potent the hammers rumble.
The hammers rumble. Their rude symphony
shows me the compact energy of the physical.

In the rough silence the hammers rumble.

In the rough silence the hammers rumble.
A new music of vigorous cadence.
Music that with masculine strength reveals
the rigid grandeur of the proletarian spirit.

In the rough silence the hammers rumble.

(Translated by María Arrillaga)

Red Christ

Beyond the towers
enlivened by the flight of birds
there is a cross, and a man nailed to the cross.
It is you, red Christ.
You are not born in the castle soft with carpets,
red Christ.
Nor is the man of the ivory and amber cigarette he who
begets you.
The mass begets you,
the mass foaming with Christs,
the mass of sweat, of weeping and of blood,

la masa que se perfila como un monte
y que, en espasmo de centurias,
se raja y lanza su corazón a la inmensidad.
Cristo rojo, tus melenas destilan Aldebaranes
y en tus ojos aúlla lo que tiene de divino el hombre.
Tus ojos hablan de Vía Crucis de milenios.
Tus ojos hablan del dolor de todos, Cristo de admoniciones, Cristo de rebeldías.
Tus manos, Cristo rojo, están empolvadas de polvo de diamantes.
Tus manos zanjadas y negras, tus manos retorcidas en el barro y aumentadas por el barro;
tus manos elevadas a la luz, manchadas de cal y de tinta;
tus manos viriles, tus manos creadoras, como las del forjador de universos.

Tus pies se han deformado en los caminos.
Tus pies se han destrozado en los caminos.
Tus pies han rubricado los caminos,
y estos han pasado del gris al escarlata.
Yo te hablo a ti, Mesías del bronce y del granito,
angustiado como el planeta y profundo como el cielo.
Los trabajadores y los luchadores, los sufrientes y los temerarios, están en ti, Cristo rojo.

Cristo social, Cristo obrero,
desenterrador del oro y buscador de la perla,
tú arrancas a la tierra y al mar sus tesoros,
y los explotadores te arrancan a ti la vida: tu tesoro.
En las planicies, donde el arado clava su diente;
en los bosques, donde el hacha se desnuda y brilla;
en las fraguas, donde el hierro es batido sobre los yunques;
en la máquina de los ferrocarriles, donde el carbón se vuelve lengua de púrpura;
dondequiera que el brazo establece su dominio,
tú te levantas para sostener el mundo.
Te pertenecen, Cristo rojo,
el terrón y la madera, el metal y el fuego.
Cristo de violencia,
Cristo hermano del Cristo de los suaves futuros,

the mass showing its profile like a mountain
and that in a spasm of centuries,
splits open and throws its heart to the immensity.
Red Christ, your hair distills Aldebarans
and in your eyes howls whatever is divine in man.
Your eyes speak of Ways of the Cross of millenniums.
Your eyes speak of the collective pain, Christ of admonitions, Christ of rebellions.
Your hands, red Christ, are dusted with dust
of diamonds.
Your hands ditched and black, your hands twisted in the mud and increased by the mud;
Your hands raised to the light, stained with lime and ink:
Your virile hands, your creative hands, as those of the forger of universes.

Your feet have been deformed in the roads.
Your feet have been shattered in the roads.
Your feet have sealed the roads,
and these have passed from gray to scarlet.
I speak to you, Messiah of bronze and granite,
anguished like the planet and profound like the sky.
The workers and the fighters, the suffering and the reckless are in you, red Christ.

Social Christ, worker Christ,
unearther of the gold, seeker of the pearl,
you pluck the treasures from the earth and from the sea,
and the exploiters take your life: your treasure.
In the plains, where the plow sinks its teeth;
in the woods, where the ax is naked and glimmers:
in the forges, where iron is subdued over the anvils;
in the machinery of the railroads, where coal becomes a purple tongue;
wherever the arm establishes its domain
you rise to sustain the world.
They belong to you, red Christ,
the soil and the wood, metal and fire.
Christ of violence,
Christ brother of the Christ of gentle futures,

tú tampoco tienes una piedra donde reclinar
la frente
coronada de eternidades.
Cristo rojo, tú has ganado la mejor batalla
desde el Calvario de los grandes esfuerzos.
Te crucifican en las carreteras y en los andamios,
te crucifican en las granjas y en los muelles,
te crucifican en las imprentas y en las redacciones de los periódicos,
te crucifican en las trincheras y en el aire,
te crucifican con los clavos que tú mismo
produces,
Cristo tallador de multitudes,
Cristo propulsor de multitudes,
Cristo entrañado en las multitudes que se afanan, se estrujan, y ruedan
con andrajos, pústulas y livideces.
Cristo del músculo y del espíritu.
Cristo que consumes tu mocedad briosa
en el titánico empuje de reconstruir el mundo
y que ignoras el instante en que has de ser relegado
como las herramientas inutilizadas por la herrumbre.
Cristo rojo, Cristo rojo,
Cristo que oyes llorar a las mujeres y a los niños hechos de tu carne,
despréndete de la cruz en que estás clavado
y avanza, avanza, avanza.
Asciende en el hervor del día nuevo.
El alba abre ya los horizontes,
y mas allá de los horizontes
se proyecta tu sombra, Cristo rojo.

you don't have a stone either, where you may rest
your brow
crowned with eternities.
Red Christ, you have won the best battle
from the Calvary of the great efforts.
They crucify you on the roads and on the scaffolds,
They crucify you in the farms and in the wharfs,
They crucify you in the printing shops and in the newspaper offices,
They crucify you in the trenches and in the air,
They crucify you with the nails that you yourself
manufacture,
Christ carver of multitudes,
Christ propeller of multitudes,
Christ entrailed in the multitudes that toil, are crushed,
that roll
with rags, scabs, and livid faces.
Christ of the muscle and the spirit.
Christ consuming your vigorous youth
in the titanic effort of reconstructing the world
and ignoring the instant when you will be forgotten
like the tools made useless by oxidation.
Red Christ, red Christ,
Christ, you who listen to the women and children made
of your flesh crying,
come down from the cross where you are nailed
and advance, advance, advance.
Climb up in the heat of the new day.
The dawn already opens new horizons,
and beyond the horizons,
red Christ, we see the outline of your shadow.

(Translated by María Arrillaga)

Juan Antonio Corretjer (b. 1908)

Pero a pesar de todo

Cuando yo vine
—cabeza desnuda, ojos en el vacío, manecitas tiernas—
encontré una casona amplia
en donde la luz del sol entraba
y el viento removía descuidos de mi hermana.
Era en ese sitio ancho que tiene el cielo arriba
y abajo mariposas, flores, hortalizas.
Después fueron mis pies dos cabritos ariscos
y mis manos dos aves entre las flores y las frutas.
Más tarde, me calzaron la hombría
y hasta un papel con la enredadera de mi nombre
en la pared atónita de la alcoba.
Entonces me separaron del río, de mi caballo,
de mi rifle y mis canciones.
Mi porvenir era, en una mente ingenua,
unos años de ausencia
y una transformación en el regreso . . .
epílogo: ceremonioso paseo hasta la iglesia.
Pero ah, empecé a fotografiar horizontes
y a imprimir quimeras.
Sobre la mesa del dolor del mundo
edité mi proyecto de vida.
Vi el florido sendero de una dulce existencia de familia,
adornado con tiestos de claudicaciones.
Un tierno antesdeayer me enviaba
a repetirme. Con los brazos abiertos,
hogar—tranquilidad, esposa, hijos—esperaba . . .
Pero a pesar de todo he preferido esto . . .
No habrá boda en el pueblo.
No tirará, sobre los tejados, piedrecitas alegres, la
  campana.
Ni habrá vino en la mesa,

But in Spite of Everything

When I came
—naked head, eyes in a vacuum, tender hands—
I found a large house
where the sunlight entered
and the wind shifted my sister's oversights.
It was in that wide place that had the sky above
and butterflies, flowers, and green plants below.
Later my feet became two skittish goats,
and my hands two birds among the flowers and the fruits.
Much later, they fitted me with manhood
and even a role with the twining of my name
on the astonished bedroom wall.
Then they separated me from the river, from my horse,
from my rifle and my songs.
My livelihood was, in a candid mind,
some years of absence
and a transformation upon returning . . .
epilogue: ceremonial walk to the church.
But oh, I started photographing horizons
and printing fantasies.
On the table of the world's pain
I edited my life's work.
I saw the flowered path of a sweet family existence,
decorated with pots of claudications.
A sweet day-before-yesterday sent
me to repeat myself. With open arms,
I waited—tranquillity, wife, children—for a home. . . .
But in spite of everything I have preferred this. . . .
There will be no wedding in town.
The bell won't throw happy stones over the tiled
roofs
There will be no wine on the table,

ni caracolearán sonrisas en traje de domingo en la jarana.
Como ropa tendida, un mundo se ha caído por la ventana.
Pero tengo una felicidad más mía, más de todos,
porque es también de todos la desgracia.
Ahora soy
un cajón en una esquina
y muchas voces juntas maldiciendo la tiranía.
Ahora soy tan solo un buen muchacho . . .
Para todos, menos para la policía . . .

AVISO:
A quien interese el desenlace
que lo busque en la prensa . . . cualquier día.

Días grandes

Miércoles de ceniza.
Regis Debray escucha
rezar a los gorilas.

Día de reyes.
El "Ché"
triunfa en Santa Clara.
Camilo va a Colombia.
Fidel entra en la Habana.
¡Hosanna!

Sábado de gloria.
Sobre la arena de Playa Girón
oído por radio visto por televisión
¡oh!
¡el tío samuel es todo un maricón!

nor whirlpool smiles in Sunday dress at the dance.
As clothes are hung, so a world has fallen out the window.
But I have happiness more mine, more of everyone's,
because the misfortune is everyone's.
I am now
a box on a corner
and many voices together cursing tyranny.
I am now merely a good boy. . . .
For all, except the police. . . .

ANNOUNCEMENT:
Whoever is interested in the ending
look for it in the papers . . . any day.

(Translated by Digna Sánchez-Méndez)

Great Days

Ash Wednesday.
Regis Debray listens
to the gorillas praying.

Three Kings' Day.
Che
triumphs in Santa Clara.
Camilo goes to Colombia.
Fidel enters Havana.
Hosanna!

Easter Saturday.
On the sand of the Bay of Pigs
heard over the radio seen on television
Oh!
Uncle Sam is all faggot!

(Translated by Digna Sánchez-Méndez)

Francisco Matos Paoli (b. 1915)

Pedro se llama el Dirigente.

Pedro se llama el Dirigente.

Piedra de Puerto Rico, piedra fluvial y
alada
con el aroma de la sangre mártir
de un Domingo de Ramos.

Delante de él la fuerza es imposible.

Por más que agitamos las manos
no podemos coger el rocío.

Está lejos el sueño
en el reino de la lógica,
en la maldad del hielo que crepita hasta vencer
esta infiel y aparente norma de la tierra.

Tenemos que enloquecer,
extraer de nosotros mismos la raíz despavorida
del cielo,
volcar nuestras miradas fatigantes,
quedar solos con una extraña soledad acompañada,
con los vigías tan terribles
que exigen el precio de la sangre
para anudar los ruiseñores
en la brama potente de la luz
que viene de los Tres Picachos.

Yo sé que el Inocente seduce.

Cae primero, pero es un caer
engañoso,
desciende primero,

The Leader's Name Is Pedro

The leader's name is Pedro.

Stone of Puerto Rico, stone of the rivers and the fluttering wings
with the aroma of martyr's blood
of a Palm Sunday.

Before him strength is impossible.

No matter how much we move our hands
we can't get the dew.

The dream is far away
in the kingdom of logic,
in the wickedness of ice which crackles until it defeats
this unfaithful and apparent norm of earth.

We have to become insane,
and extract from ourselves the terrified root
of heaven,
overturn our tired looks,
remain alone with a strange accompanied solitude,
with watchtowers so terrible
that they demand the price of blood
to knot nightingales
in the strong roar of the light
that comes from Tres Picachos.

I know that the Innocent one seduces.

He falls first, but it's a deceiving
fall,
descends first,

pero después ondula
en mitad de la sien tan constelada de la sangre.

Cesaría yo
si el Inocente no me respondiera
cuando el camino vierte su impotencia
en todos los nacidos de la llama.

Biografía de un poeta

Estuve un tiempo en jaulas
de nieblas, sedimentos, chispas, lirios
fugaces. No llamaba
nadie. Ni la luz era la luz,
desnacido por siempre en blanca aldea
lejana. Muchos niños
detenían los astros para arder
en los nuncas. La mano, ya preñada
de oclusión, no cogía
las margaritas, leves cielos
caídos. El ausente
habitaba los ecos,
vivía por detrás del horizonte,
sin conocer las llamas
del crepúsculo impío.
Después, vino el martirio.
El aire, ya ternura
de mí, se colmó de silencios
furtivos. La montaña,
con su verde vivaz,
recogió la extrañeza de los años
en el extremo albor de la armonía.
Entonces, cuántas manos
apretando la niebla,
cuántos saludos de rojez
campesina. Vine al mundo:
la semilla parió a todo un hombre,

but later undulates
in the middle of the temple so starred with blood.

Would I stop
if the Innocent didn't answer me
when the road inverts its impotence
in all the births from the flame.

(Translated by Digna Sánchez-Méndez)

Biography of a Poet

For a while I was in cages
of clouds, sediments, sparks, brief
lilies. Didn't call
anyone. Not even the light was light,
forever unborn in a far-off
white hamlet. Many children
stopped the astros in order to burn
in the nothings. The hand, already pregnant
from occlusion, didn't pick
the daisies, brief heavens
fallen. The absent one
inhabited the echoes,
lived behind the horizon,
without knowing the flames
of the impious twilight.
Later came martyrdom.
The air, already tender
with me, was filled by furtive
silences. The mountain,
with its green liveliness,
gathered the strangeness of the years
in the extreme whiteness of harmony.
Then, how many hands
pressing the cloud,
how many red peasant
greetings. I came to the world:
the seed gave birth to a whole man,

a un dios ya conocido
que destrozaba la camándula
del recuerdo. Abertura
del alma que se puebla
de todas las fragancias de la tierra.

Democracia

Un silencio ominoso
acicalado de cadenas
multiplica rodillas
en la desierta arena de los tránsfugas.
Un silencio de piedra
que se fabrica lejos,
abierto a los hipócritas
en palabras, palabras y palabras.
Un silencio de hambre
en que los pordioseros
comen despavoridos
el suculento plato de la nada.
Un silencio de pus
mecido por la guerra
que condecora héroes
sin mirada,
que convierte la sangre
en la sucia moneda de los parias.
Un silencio total de mundo libre
regido por plutócratas
donde todo se vende:
la vergüenza, el rocío, las entrañas.
Un silencio
que llaga
la boca
con mordazas.
Un silencio de miedos ancestrales
que suspende del aire

a god already known
who destroyed the bead
of memory. Opening
of the soul which is populated
by all the fragrances of the earth.

(Translated by Digna Sánchez-Méndez)

Democracy

An ominous silence
polished by chains
multiplies knees
in the desert sand of the fugitives.
A stone silence
made far away
open to the hypocrites
in words, words and words.
A silence of hunger
where the beggars
eat horrified
a succulent plate of nothingness.
A silence of pus
swung by the war
that decorates heroes
without looks,
which turns blood
into dirty coins of the pariahs.
A total silence of the free world,
governed by plutocrats,
where everything is sold:
shame, dew, entrails.
A silence
that scabs
the mouth
with muzzles.
A silence of ancestral fears
which suspends the puppets

los títeres
en nombre de la patria.
Un silencio que aísla, que corroe,
que despuebla, que mancha.
Un silencio rodeado
por las bombas atómicas
donde se oculta el sol hasta la náusea.
Un silencio de esclavos:
se llama democracia.

La muerte de Dios

Cortina. Dura cortina
de lo que es alboreado.
Cerrado el viejo candado,
la incandescencia supina.

De momento, la teoría
de tempestad tan absorta.
El diamante en ira. Importa
no tener más alegría.

¿Por qué huye el peregrino?
Es obsoleta su estancia.
Ya como que no hay fragancia
para verter este vino.

El Dios muerto. La palabra
tendida. Yo no despierto
en el alba. Muro yerto
en la ilusión que se labra.

Cortina. Ya se detiene
el relámpago fortuito.
Dios finito, muy finito.
Envuelto en polvo, no viene.

in the air
in the name of the country.
A silence that isolates, that corrodes,
that depopulates, that stains.
A silence surrounded
by the atomic bombs
where the sun hides until nauseous.
A silence of slaves:
it is called democracy.

(Translated by Digna Sánchez-Méndez)

The Death of God

Curtain. Hard curtain
of what is dawned.
The old lock closed,
supine incandescence.

Suddenly, so amazed
the tempest theory.
The diamond in anger. It matters
not to have more happiness.

Why does the pilgrim flee?
His staying is obsolete.
Now no longer is there fragrance
to spill this wine.

The dead God. The word
rested. I no longer awaken
at dawn. Stiff rampart
that's made in illusion.

Curtain. Already the unexpected
lightning detains itself.
Finite God, very finite.
Wrapped in dust, He doesn't come.

Traiciona hasta el bello monte.
Traiciona el azul baldío.
Porque ahogado está en el río
por detrás del horizonte.

El Dios muerto. Lancinante
como pena retenida.
No hay almas. En la partida
el hombre recio y distante.

Cortina. Negror. Incienso
disoluto. Rito frío
que no tiene poderío
para el fuego en que me pienso.

Blasfemia. La nada en perla.
El ser trocado en pavura.
Solamente la figura
para jamás entreverla.

Asesino. Sangre pide
la estrella falsa. Asesino
porque no existe el camino
para el pie que no coincide.

Sopor en el mar silente.
Cortina. Abortado cielo
que renuncia a su consuelo
en lo impío de la mente.

Así el vacío: la gloria
que no cumple con el alba.
El Dios muerto no se salva.
Ha perdido trayectoria.

El espectro no fulmina.
Y el placer ya se amamanta.
El Dios muerto no adelanta.
Cortina. Dura cortina.

Betrays even the beautiful mountain.
Betrays the empty blue.
Because he's drowned in the river
behind the horizon.

The dead God. Lancing
like sadness kept in.
There are no souls. In passing away
man is strong and distant.

Curtain. Blackness. Dissipated
incense. Cold rite
which has no power
for the fire in which I think myself.

Blasphemy. Nothingness pearled.
Your being changed to fear.
Only the figure
never to see her.

Assassin. The false star
asks for blood. Assassin
because the road doesn't exist
for the foot that doesn't coincide.

Drowsiness in a tranquil sea.
Curtain. Aborted sky
which renounces its comfort
in the impiety of the mind.

Thus the vacuum: the glory
which doesn't come through with the dawn.
The dead God can't save himself.
He has lost his trajectory.

The specter doesn't fulminate.
And pleasure already suckles itself.
The dead God doesn't advance.
Curtain. Hard curtain.

(Translated by Digna Sánchez-Méndez)

Part Two

THE MAJOR POETS

Luis Palés Matos (1898–1959)

Bocetos impresionistas

I

Vamos, acróbatas modernos,
sobre trapecio de metáforas
a hacer maromas peligrosas
para que el gran público aplauda.
Saco imágenes del bolsillo
como rosas recién cortadas . . .
Heme aquí, de pie en el trapecio,
disparado en mecida larga
hacia la flor que no perfuma,
hacia la estrella que no existe,
hacia el pájaro que no canta.

II

Ese árbol seco
comido de lianas y helechos,
es como el viejo zapatero
siempre enredado entre zapatos
que ahora, de repente, recuerdo . . .
vidas iguales, frías, áridas,
y en torno la llanura
abierta en dilatado bostezo.

III

El buen marido esta mañana
dice a su mujer: —Prepara
las maletas, que voy de viaje—.
Ella lo mira de tal modo
que él comprende, lía un cigarrillo,
y lanza una espiral dolorosa de humo.

Impressionistic Sketches

I

Let's do dangerous stunts,
modern acrobats,
upon a trapeze of metaphors
so the great public will applaud.
I take images out of my pocket
like freshly cut roses . . .
Here I am, standing on the trapeze,
flying in a long swing
toward the flower that doesn't smell,
toward the star that doesn't exist,
toward the bird that doesn't sing.

II

That dry tree
eaten by vines and ferns,
is like the old shoemaker
always entangled among shoes
that now, suddenly, I remember . . .
the same lives, cold, arid
and round about the plain
open in a drawn-out yawn.

III

This morning the good husband
says to his wife: "Prepare
my luggage; I'm going away."
She looks at him in such a way
that he understands, rolls a cigarette
and exhales a painful spiral of smoke.

IV

Ni el tranvía, ni el teatro, ni el cabaret pudieron
extirpar la yerba, los árboles y el agua
que aquel hombre llevaba
en la risa, en el chaleco y en la corbata,
y así, aquel hombre era,
una pradera suelta por las calles.

V

Tierra de hambres y saqueos
y de poetas y azucareros . . .
Antilla perfumada que arrastra
su estómago vacío sobre el agua.
Jaula de loros tropicales
politiqueando entre los árboles.
¡Pobre isla donde yo he nacido!
El yanki, bull-dog negro,
te roe entre sus patas como un hueso.

VI

Tendido boca arriba
me arropo con el cielo
en la noche del trópico
silbante, murmurioso y trompetero.
Tendido boca arriba
en cósmica expansión me voy abriendo
mientras el sueño cierra mis pupilas.
Mas de pronto despierto
con una extraña comezón de mundos,
y miro las estrellas
que como chinches andan por mi cuerpo.

VII

En esta hora quieta
de la bahía ancha,
la tarde es puerto sosegado
de penumbra y de calma . . .
La noche entra como un gran navío
y arroja sobre el agua
su primera estrella
como un ancla.

IV

Not the streetcar, nor the theater, nor the cabaret could
uproot the grass, the trees and the water
which that man carried
in his laughter, in his vest and in his necktie,
and so, that man was
a meadow set free on the streets.

V

Land of hunger and pillage
and of poets and sugar barons . . .
Perfumed Antilles that drags
its empty stomach on the water.
Cage of tropical parrots
politicking amid the trees
Poor island where I was born!
The yankee, black bulldog,
gnaws on you like a bone between his feet.

VI

Lying on my back
I cover myself with the sky
in the tropical night
whistling, murmuring and trumpeting.
Lying on my back
I open up in cosmic expansion
while sleep closes my pupils.
But suddenly I awake
with a strange itching of worlds,
and look at the stars
that crawl over my body like bedbugs.

VII

In this quiet hour
of the wide bay,
the afternoon is a peaceful port
of shadow and calm . . .
Night enters like a great ship
and throws upon the water
its first star
as an anchor.

(Translated by Ellen G. Matilla)

Voz de lo sedentario y lo monótono

Días iguales—largos como caras sombrías
de señores que llegan a casa de visita,
y hablan, tiesos, de vagas ciudades destruidas,
de templos demolidos y éxodos de familias.

Días hostiles. Salir de una estéril vigilia
con los ojos hinchados por la bohemia vampira.
Un amargo sabor en la boca y neblina
en el cerebro para pensar sobre la vida.

Ir al correo. Ver gente toda desconocida
que discute la guerra, y jadear de fatiga
ante el automatismo de las posturas rígidas
del doctor, del letrado y del comisionista.

Días . . . Las calles anchas bajo el sol aturdidas.
El polvo entre las ruedas de coches y tranvías.
Una mujer que pasa perfumada y altiva,
y al fin—¡al fin!—un perro con sarna: poesía.

Y estarse soñoliento sentado en una silla
del café de alcoholes y de negras bebidas,
y estarse, así, con ganas de emigrar . . . ¡qué fatiga!
¿Cuándo brotará el alba sonora de otro día?

*

Noches de ojo de buho que en la sombra se afila.
Aúllan los perros negros en la montaña lívida,
en las encrucijadas los crímenes meditan
y se abren los prostíbulos y las hoscas garitas.

Alcohol y lujuria. Y la carne crepita.
La carne, ese fermento de manzana podrida.
La soledad absorbe como esponja vacía,
y abajo, un gusanero de miseria, y arriba . . .

Sounds of Stagnance and Monotony

Same days—long like somber faces
of men who come to visit,
talking stiffly of vague cities now destroyed,
of demolished temples and family migrations.

Hostile days. To come out of a futile wake
with eyes swollen by the sting of the bohemian vampire.
A bitter taste in the mouth and mist
in the brain when thinking about life.

The post office. To see all unknown people
who discuss war, and to part with fatigue
before the automatism of the rigid positions
of the doctor, the lawyer and the salesman.

Days . . . The wide streets numb under the sun.
Dust among the wheels of cars and streetcars.
A woman who passes perfumed and proud,
and at the end—finally—a mangy dog: poetry.

And, drowsy, to remain seated in a chair
in the café of alcohol and somber drinks
and to be, like that, wanting to leave . . . what weariness!
When will the resonant dawn of another day toll?

*

Owl-eyed nights that sharpen in the shadow.
Black dogs howl on the pale mountain,
crimes meditate at crossroads
while brothels and gambling joints open.

Alcohol and lust. And the flesh crackling.
Flesh, that ferment of rotten apples.
Solitude absorbs like an empty sponge,
and below, a worm nest of misery, and above . . .

Translated from *Luis Palés Matos, Poesía 1915–1956,* University of Puerto Rico Press, 4th ed., 1971.

Insomnio de murciélago de esa poetería
que lleva sobre el pecho una llaga encendida.
Las horas caen aisladas, como gotas letíferas
de filtros que levantan viscosas pesadillas.

Noches de bandoleros y prostitutas tísicas.
Sangra el pulmón enfermo y los pechos se inflan.
Sobre el viento oleoso de las calles sombrías,
la tos se abre como una doliente margarita.

Y estrujar en la cama la neurosis de avispas,
con los nervios crispados cual bruscas sabandijas,
y esperar, en un sueño de alcanfor y fatiga
el canto de la alondra que anuncia el nuevo día.

*

Iría así, de viaje, por un camino inter-
minable, en un cupé largo, pesado y gris.
Y jadear el cansancio del caballo y tener
la remota visión de un lejano país.

Y mirar las llanuras secas de hojas y cañas,
y el crepúsculo húmedo como una flor postrera,
y sentir la carroña senil de las montañas
en un reflorar tardo de oscura primavera.

¡Oh pueblo gris y opaco! —città morta—diría
D'Annunzio. Gente oscura y densa, de sombrías
pasiones. Resolanas inmóviles, y rígidas
tertulias de honorables señores de botica.

¿Pero cómo yo pude vivir aquí? ¿Qué línea
sedentaria y monótona pudo tirar mi vida;
y cómo en esta aldea chata, feroz y esquiva,
pudo nacer la rosa triste de mi poesía?

¡Oh pueblo gris y opaco! Santiago Rusiñol.
(Una calle de cal bajo el terrible fuego
solar. En la botica, conservada en alcohol
una tenia: ¡la única notoriedad del pueblo!)

The batlike insomnia of those poets
who carry a burning wound on their chests.
The hours fall isolated, like milky drops
of philtres that raise viscous nightmares.

Nights of bandits and consumptive whores.
The diseased lung bleeds, and the breasts swell.
Over the oily wind of gloomy streets,
Cough opens like an aching daisy.

And to crush in bed the wasplike neurosis
with nerves on edge like coarse reptiles,
and in a dream of camphor and fatigue await
the song of the lark that heralds the new day.

*

I would go like that, on a trip, by a never-
ending road, in a long coupé, heavy and gray.
And panting the fatigue of the horse, have
the distant vision of a faraway land.

And to see the dry plains of leaves and cane,
and the humid dusk like a lingering flower,
and to feel the senile carrion of the mountains
in a belated reflowering of black spring.

Oh gray and opaque town "*Città morta*" as D'Annunzio
would say. Dark and dense people, of somber
passions. Immobile glare and rigid
gatherings of honorable drugstore gentlemen.

But how could I live here? What stagnant
and monotonous thread could trace my life;
and how could in this flattened, fierce and elusive village
the sad rose of my poetry bloom?

Oh gray and opaque town! Santiago Rusiñol
(A limestone street under the terrible solar
fire. In the drugstore, preserved in alcohol
a tapeworm: the only news in town!)

¡Oh el deleite enfermizo de estar convaleciente
de una larga parálisis en un jardín riente,
y escuchar como una música muy lejana
las voces cariñosas de la madre y la hermana!

¡Estaría tan inmóvil en mi sillón de ruedas!
¡Habría tanta fiesta de sol por las veredas
del jardín, que hasta gracias al Señor le daría
por mis piernas inválidas y mi vida baldía!

Luego viene una amiga de mi hermana a indagar.
—¿Cómo sigue el enfermo? ¿Aún no puede andar?—
Y mi hermana, mirándome con velado temor,
diría lo de siempre: —Hoy se encuentra mejor . . .

—Hoy me siento mejor, sí—. Yo, con mi ironía
rencorosa de inválido también respondería;
presintiendo que nunca me podré levantar
de mi sillón de ruedas . . . Un ansia de llorar,

larga, eterna, profunda, me oprime el corazón.
Pero ¡bah! esto no es nada. Doy un brusco empujón
a mi amigo que gusta rodar por las veredas,
y allá voy, como siempre, en mi sillón de ruedas.

El llamado

Me llaman desde allá . . .
larga voz de hoja seca,
mano fugaz de nube
que en el aire de otoño se dispersa.
Por arriba el llamado
tira de mí con tenue hilo de estrella,
abajo, el agua en tránsito,
con sollozo de espuma entre la niebla.

Oh, the sickly delight of recovering
in a laughing garden, from a long paralysis
hearing, as very distant music
the affectionate voices of mother and sister.

I would be so still in my wheelchair!
There would be so many sun feasts in the
paths of the garden that I would even thank the Lord
for my crippled legs and my barren life.

Later a friend of my sister comes to inquire.
"How is the patient? Can he walk yet?"
And my sister, watching me with veiled fear,
would say as always: "Today he feels better . . ."

"Today I feel better, yes." Me, with the spiteful
irony of an invalid would also say;
foreboding that I will never rise again
from my wheelchair . . . A desire to cry,

long, eternal, profound, oppresses my heart.
But, ah, this is nothing. I give a brusque push
to my friend who likes to roll along the paths
and there I go, as always, in my wheelchair.

(Translated by Ellen G. Matilla)

The Call

They are calling me from beyond . . .
long voice of dried leaf,
fleeting hand of cloud
that is dispersed in the autumn air.
From above, the call
pulls at me with a tenuous thread of stars;
below, the moving waters
with sobs of foam through the mist.

Translated from *Luis Palés Matos, Poesía 1915–1956,* University of Puerto Rico Press, 4th ed., 1971.

Ha tiempo oigo las voces
y descubro las señas.

Hoy recuerdo: es un día venturoso
de cielo despejado y clara tierra;
golondrinas erráticas
el calmo azul puntean.
Estoy frente a la mar y en lontananza
se va perdiendo el ala de una vela;
va yéndose, esfumándose,
y yo también me voy borrando en ella.
Y cuando al fin retorno
por un leve resquicio de conciencia
¡cuán lejos ya me encuentro de mí mismo!
¡qué mundo más extraño me rodea!

Ahora, dormida junto a mí, reposa
mi amor sobre la hierba.
El seno palpitante
sube y baja tranquilo en la marea
del ímpetu calmado que diluye
espectrales añiles en su ojera.
Miro esa dulce fábrica rendida,
cuerpo de trampa y presa
cuyo ritmo esencial como jugando
manufactura la caricia aérea,
el arrullo narcótico y el beso
—víspera ardiente de gozosa queja—
y me digo: Ya todo ha terminado . . .
Mas de pronto, despierta,
y allá en el negro hondón de sus pupilas
que son un despedirse y una ausencia,
algo me invita a su remota margen
y dulcemente, sin querer, me lleva.

Me llaman desde allá . . .
Mi nave aparejada está dispuesta,
a su redor, en grumos de silencio,
sordamente coagula la tiniebla.
Un mar hueco, sin peces,

For a long time I have heard the voices
and discovered the signs.

Today I remember: it is a halcyon day
of cloudless sky and clear ground;
erratic swallows
stipple the quiet blue.
I am facing the sea and in the distance
the wing of a sail is disappearing;
it's leaving, vanishing,
and I, too, dissolving in it.
And when I finally return
through a last crevice of consciousness,
how far I find me from myself!
What a strange world surrounds me!

Now, asleep by me my love
rests upon the grass.
Tranquil, the pulsing breast
ebbs and flows in the tide
of the satisfied wants that dilute
ghostly bluing under her eyes.
I look at this gentle exhausted factory,
body of trap and prey
whose essential rhythm, as if playing,
manufactures the airy caress,
the narcotic lullaby and the kiss
—burning eve of joyful complaint—
and I say to myself: "It's all over now."
But suddenly she awakens
and there in the black chasm of her eyes
that are a farewell and an absence
something invites me to their remote edge
and sweetly, without warning, carries me.

They are calling me from beyond . . .
My rigged ship is ready;
surrounding it, in clusters of silence,
darkness deafly coagulates.
A hollow sea, without fish,

agua vacía y negra
sin vena de fulgor que la penetre
ni pisada de brisa que la mueva.
Fondo inmóvil de sombra,
límite gris de piedra . . .
¡Oh soledad, que a fuerza de andar sola
se siente de sí misma compañera!

*

Emisario solícito que vienes
con oculto mensaje hasta mi puerta,
sé lo que te propones
y no me engaña tu misión secreta;
me llaman desde allá,
pero el amor dormido aquí en la hierba
es bello todavía
y un júbilo de sol baña la tierra.
¡Déjeme tu implacable poderío
una hora, un minuto más con ella!

Kalahari

¿Por qué ahora la palabra Kalahari?

El día es hermoso y claro. En la luz bailotean
con ágil gracia, seres luminosos y alegres:
el pájaro, la brizna de hierba, las cantáridas,
y las moscas que en vuelo redondo y embriagado
rebotan contra el limpio cristal de mi ventana.
A veces una nube blanca lo llena todo
con su mole rolliza, hinchada, bombonosa,
y en despliegue adiposo de infladura
es como un imponente pavo real del cielo.

black and empty water
without a vein of light that penetrates it
nor a step of wind to stir it.
Immobile depth of shadow,
stone-gray limit . . .
Oh solitude, so often alone that she
feels like a companion to herself.

*

Solicitous emissary, you come
with a concealed message to my door;
I know what you want
and I'm not fooled by your secret mission;
they are calling me from beyond,
but love asleep here on the grass
is beautiful still
and a joyful sun bathes the earth.
Let your implacable power allow me
an hour, one more minute with her!

(Translated by Ellen G. Matilla)

Kalahari

Why now the word *Kalahari*?

The day is clear and beautiful—under the sunlight
bright and cheery beings dance with agile grace:
the bird, the blade of grass, the blister beetles,
and the flies in a round drunken flight
bounce against the clean glass of my window.
Sometimes a white cloud fills up everything
with its plump swollen cotton candy
and in its adipose puffed-up display
is like an imposing peacock of the sky.

¿Por qué ahora la palabra Kalahari?

Anoche estuve de francachela con los amigos,
y derivamos hacia un lupanar absurdo
allá por el sombrío distrito de los muelles . . .
El agua tenebrosa ponía un vaho crudo
de marisco, y el viento ondulaba premioso
a través de los tufos peculiares del puerto.
En el burdel reían estrepitosamente
las mujeres de bocas pintadas . . . Sin embargo,
una, inmóvil, callaba; callaba sonreída,
y se dejaba hacer sonreída y callada.
Estaba ebria. Las cosas sucedían distantes.
Recuerdo que alguien dijo –Camella, un trago, un trago.

¿Por qué ahora la palabra Kalahari?

Esta mañana, hojeando un magazín de cromos,
ante un perrillo de aguas con cinta roja al cuello,
estuve largo tiempo observando, observando . . .
No sé por qué mi pensamiento a la deriva
fondeó en una bahía de claros cocoteros,
con monos, centenares de monos que trenzaban
una desordenada cadena de cabriolas.

¿Por qué ahora la palabra Kalahari?

Ha surgido de pronto, inexplicablemente . . .
¡Kalahari! ¡Kalahari! ¡Kalahari!
¿De dónde habrá surgido esta palabra
escondida como un insecto en mi memoria;
picada como una mariposa disecada
en la caja de coleópteros de mi memoria,
y ahora viva, insistiendo, revoloteando ciega
contra la luz ofuscadora del recuerdo?
¡Kalahari! ¡Kalahari! ¡Kalahari!

¿Por qué ahora la palabra Kalahari?

Why now the word *Kalahari*?

Last night I did the town with friends,
and came to an absurd brothel
over by the gloomy district of the docks.
The murky water exuded a raw smell of shellfish,
and the wind billowed tightly
through the peculiar odors of the harbor.
In the bordel, the women with painted mouths
laughed boisterously . . . yet one,
still, was silent; silently smiling,
and she abandoned herself smiling and silent.
She was drunk. Things happened in the distance.
I remember someone saying, "Camella, a drink, a drink."

Why now the word *Kalahari*?

This morning, leafing through a magazine with photos,
I stopped for a long time at one of a little spaniel
with a red collar around his neck, gazing, gazing . . .
I don't know why my drifting thoughts
cast anchor in a bay of bright coconut palms,
with monkeys, hundreds of monkeys, braiding
a disorderly chain of capers.

Why now the word *Kalahari*?

It has come forth suddenly, inexplicably . . .
"Kalahari! Kalahari! Kalahari!"
Where can it have come from, this word
concealed like an insect in my memory;
impaled like a mounted butterfly
in the beetlebox of my memory,
and now alive, insisting, blindly fluttering
against the bewildering light of recollections?
"Kalahari! Kalahari! Kalahari!"

Why now the word *Kalahari*?

(Translated by Diego de la Texera)

Ñam-ñam

Ñam-ñam. En la carne blanca
los dientes negros—ñam-ñam.
Las tijeras de las bocas
sobre los muslos—ñam-ñam.
Van y vienen las quijadas
con sordo ritmo—ñam-ñam.
La feroz noche deglute
bosques y junglas—ñam-ñam.

Ñam-ñam. Africa mastica
en el silencio—ñam-ñam,
su cena de exploradores
y misioneros—ñam-ñam.
Quien penetró en Tangañica
por vez primera—ñam-ñam;
quien llegó hasta Tembandumba
la gran matriarca—ñam-ñam.

Ñam-ñam. Los fetiches abren
sus bocas negras—ñam-ñam.
En las pupilas del brujo
un solo fulgor—ñam-ñam.
La sangre del sacrificio
embriaga el tótem—ñam-ñam,
y Nigricia es toda dientes
en la tiniebla—ñam-ñam.

Asia sueña su nirvana.
América baila el jazz.
Europa juega y teoriza.
Africa gruñe: ñam-ñam.

Ñam-ñam

Ñam-ñam. On white flesh
Black teeth–ñam-ñam.
The shears of the mouth
on haunches–ñam-ñam.
Back and forth the jawbones move
with muffled rhythm–ñam-ñam.
The ferocious night swallows
woods and jungles–ñam-ñam.

Ñam-ñam. Africa chews
in the silence–ñam-ñam
her supper of missionaries
and explorers–ñam-ñam.
He who first entered
Tanganyika–ñam-ñam;
he who reached Tembandumba,
the great matriarch–ñam-ñam.

Ñam-ñam. The fetishes open
their black mouths–ñam-ñam.
In the witchdoctor's pupils
a single radiance–ñam-ñam.
The blood of sacrifice
intoxicates the totem–ñam-ñam,
and Blackland is all teeth
inside the shadows–ñam-ñam.

Asia dreams on her Nirvana.
America dances jazz.
Europe gambles and theorizes.
Africa grunts: ñam-ñam.

(Translated by Diego de la Texera)

Elegía del Duque de la Mermelada

¡Oh mi fino, mi melado Duque de la Mermelada!
¿Dónde están tus caimanes en el lejano aduar del Pongo,
y la sombra azul y redonda de tus baobabs africanos,
y tus quince mujeres olorosas a selva y a fango?

Ya no comerás el suculento asado de niño,
ni el mono familiar, a la siesta, te matará los piojos,
ni tu ojo dulce rastreará el paso de la jirafa afeminada
a través del silencio plano y caliente de las sabanas.

Se acabaron tus noches con su suelta cabellera de
fogatas
y su gotear soñoliento y perenne de tamboriles,
en cuyo fondo te ibas hundiendo como en un lodo tibio
hasta llegar a las márgenes últimas de tu gran
bisabuelo.

Ahora, en el molde vistoso de tu casaca francesa,
pasas azucarado de saludos como un cortesano cualquiera,
a despecho de tus pies que desde sus botas ducales
te gritan: —Babilongo, súbete por las cornisas del
palacio—.

¡Qué gentil va mi Duque con la Madama de Cafolé,
todo afelpado y pulcro en la onda azul de los violines,
conteniendo las manos que desde sus guantes de aristócrata
le gritan: —Babilongo, derríbala sobre ese canapé de rosa!—

Desde las márgenes últimas de tu gran bisabuelo,
a través del silencio plano y caliente de las sabanas,
¿por qué lloran tus caimanes en el lejano aduar del Pongo,
¡oh mi fino, mi melado Duque de la Mermelada!?

Elegy for the Duke of Marmalade

Oh, my fine, my honey-colored Duke of Marmalade!
Where are your alligators in the distant Pongo village,
and the round blue shadows of your African baobabs,
and your fifteen wives that smell of mud and jungle?

No longer will you eat the succulent roast of child,
nor will your familiar monkey kill your lice at siesta time,
nor your soft eyes track the step of the effeminate giraffe
across the flat, hot silence of the grasslands.

Ended are your nights with their streaming hair of
bonfires
and their sleepy perpetual trickle of timbrels,
in which depth you sank as into a warm mud
until you reached the final limits of your great
grandfather.

Now in the flaring mold of your French coat,
you pass sugared with greetings like any other courtier,
in spite of your feet which shriek to you from their
ducal boots: "Babilongo, climb up the cornices of the
palace!"

How refined goes my Duke with Madame Cafolé,
all velvety and trim on the blue wave of violins,
restraining his hands which from his gentlemanly gloves
shriek at him: "Babilongo, make her on that pink lounge!"

From the final limits of your great grandfather,
across the flat, hot silence of the grasslands,
why do your alligators weep in the distant Pongo village,
oh my fine, my honey-colored Duke of Marmalade?

(Translated by Ellen G. Matilla and Diego de la Texera)

Pueblo

¡Piedad, Señor, piedad para mi pobre pueblo
donde mi pobre gente se morirá de nada!
Aquel viejo notario que se pasa los días
en su mínima y lenta preocupación de rata;
este alcalde adiposo de grande abdomen vacuo
chapoteando en su vida tal como en una salsa;
aquel comercio lento, igual, de hace diez siglos;
estas cabras que triscan el resol de la plaza;
algún mendigo, algún caballo que atraviesa
tiñoso, gris y flaco, por estas calles anchas;
la fría y atrofiante modorra del domingo
jugando en los casinos con billar y barajas;
todo, todo el rebaño tedioso de estas vidas
en este pueblo viejo donde no ocurre nada,
todo esto se muere, se cae, se desmorona,
a fuerza de ser cómodo y de estar a sus anchas.

¡Piedad, Señor, piedad para mi pobre pueblo!
Sobre estas almas simples, desata algún canalla
que contra el agua muerta de sus vidas arroje
la piedra redentora de una insólita hazaña . . .
Algún ladrón que asalte ese Banco en la noche,
algún Don Juan que viole esa doncella casta,
algún tahur de oficio que se meta en el pueblo
y revuelva estas gentes honorables y mansas.

¡Piedad, Señor, piedad para mi pobre pueblo
donde mi pobre gente se morirá de nada!

Town

Mercy, Lord, mercy for my poor town,
where my poor people will die of nothing!
That old notary who spends his days
in his petty and minimal weasel worries.
This fleshy mayor with a great empty stomach
splashing in his life like a sauce;
that slow business, the same for ten centuries;
these goats that frolic in the glare of the plaza;
some beggar, some scabby horse,
gray and thin, who goes through these wide streets;
the cold and atrophied heaviness of Sundays,
playing billiards and cards in the casinos;
everything, all the herdlike tedium of these lives
in this old town where nothing happens.
All this dies, falls, crumbles,
with so much comfort and contentment.

Mercy, Lord, mercy for my poor town!
Over these simple souls, unleash some scoundrel
who would throw against the stagnant water of their lives
the redeeming stone of an incredible feat . . .
Some thief who would rob that Bank at night,
some Don Juan who would rape that chaste maiden,
some professional gambler who would meddle in the town
and agitate these meek and worthy people.

Mercy, Lord, mercy for my poor town,
where my poor people will die of nothing!

(Translated by Ellen G. Matilla)

Julia de Burgos (1914–1953)

A Julia de Burgos

Ya las gentes murmuran que yo soy tu enemiga
porque dicen que en verso doy al mundo tu yo.

Mienten, Julia de Burgos. Mienten, Julia de Burgos.
La que se alza en mis versos no es tu voz: es mi voz;
porque tú eres ropaje y la esencia soy yo;
y el más profundo abismo se tiende entre las dos.

Tú eres fría muñeca de mentira social,
y yo, viril destello de la humana verdad.

Tú, miel de cortesanas hipocresías; yo no;
que en todos mis poemas desnudo el corazón.

Tú eres como tu mundo, egoísta; yo no;
que todo me lo juego a ser lo que soy yo.

Tú eres sólo la grave señora señorona;
yo no; yo soy la vida, la fuerza, la mujer.

Tú eres de tu marido, de tu amo; yo no;
yo de nadie, o de todos, porque a todos, a todos,
en mi limpio sentir y en mi pensar me doy.

Tú te rizas el pelo y te pintas; yo no;
a mí me riza el viento; a mí me pinta el sol.

Tú eres dama casera, resignada, sumisa,
atada a los prejuicios de los hombres; yo no;
que yo soy Rocinante corriendo desbocado
olfateando horizontes de justicia de Dios.

To Julia de Burgos

The word is out that I am your enemy
 that in my poetry I am giving you away.

They lie, Julia de Burgos. They lie, Julia de Burgos.
That voice that rises in my poems is not yours: it is my
 voice;
you are the covering and I the essence;
and between us lies the deepest chasm.

You are the frigid doll of social falsehood,
and I, the virile sparkle of human truth.

You are honey of courtly hypocrisy, not I;
I bare my heart in all my poems.

You are selfish, like your world, not I;
I gamble everything to be what I am.

You are but the grave lady, ladylike;
not I; I am life, and strength, and I am woman.

You belong to your husband, your master, not I;
I belong to no one or to everyone, because to all, to all
I give myself in pure feelings and in my thoughts.

You curl your hair, and paint your face, not I;
I am curled by the wind, painted by the sun.

You are lady of the house, resigned and meek,
tied to the prejudices of men, not I;
smelling the horizons of the justice of God.
I am Rocinante, running headlong

(Translated by María Arrillaga)

Río Grande de Loíza

¡Río Grande de Loíza! . . . Alárgate en mi
espíritu
y deja que mi alma se pierda en tus riachuelos,
para buscar la fuente que te robó de niño
y en un ímpetu loco te devolvió al sendero.

Enróscate en mis labios y deja que te beba,
para sentirte mío por un breve momento,
y esconderte del mundo y en ti mismo esconderte,
y oir voces de asombro en la boca del viento.

Apéate un instante del lomo de la tierra,
y busca de mis ansias el íntimo secreto;
confúndete en el vuelo de mi ave fantasía,
y déjame una rosa de agua en mis ensueños.

¡Río Grande de Loíza! . . . Mi manantial, mi río,
desde que alzóme al mundo el pétalo materno;
contigo se bajaron desde las rudas cuestas,
a buscar nuevos surcos, mis pálidos anhelos;
y mi niñez fue toda un poema en el río,
y un río en el poema de mis primeros sueños.

Llegó la adolescencia. Me sorprendió la vida
prendida en lo más ancho de tu viajar eterno;
y fui tuya mil veces, y en un bello romance
me despertaste el alma y me besaste el cuerpo.

¿A dónde te llevaste las aguas que bañaron
mis formas, en espiga de sol recién abierto?

¡Quién sabe en qué remoto país mediterráneo
algún fauno en la playa me estará poseyendo!

¡Quién sabe en qué aguacero de qué tierra lejana
me estaré derramando para abrir surcos nuevos;
o si acaso, cansada de morder corazones,
me estaré congelando en cristales de hielo!

Río Grande de Loíza

Río Grande de Loíza! . . . Extend yourself into my spirit
and let my soul get lost in your streams,
to search for the fountain that stole you away as a child
and in a mad impulse returned you to the path.

Coil yourself around my lips and let me drink you,
to feel you mine for a brief moment,
and hide you from the world and hide you in yourself,
and hear astonished voices in the mouth of the wind.

Get off for an instant from the loin of the earth,
and look for the intimate secret of my longing;
lose yourself in the flight of my bird imagination,
and leave a water rose for my illusions.

Río Grande de Loíza! . . . My source, my river,
ever since the maternal petal raised me to the world;
with you went down from the rugged hills,
to look for new furrows, my pale desires;
and all my childhood was a poem in the river,
and a river in the poem of my first dreams.

Adolescence came. Life surprised me
pinned to the widest part of your eternal voyage;
and I was yours a thousand times, and in love,
you awoke my soul and kissed my body.

Where did you take the waters that bathed
my figure, with the stream of the newly risen sun?

Who knows in what remote Mediterranean country
some faun on the beach will be possessing me!

Who knows in what showers of what distant lands
I will be spilling in order to open up new furrows;
or if perhaps, tired of biting hearts,
I will be freezing in ice crystals.

¡Río Grande de Loíza! . . . Azul. Moreno. Rojo.
Espejo azul, caído pedazo azul de cielo;
desnuda carne blanca que se te vuelve negra
cada vez que la noche se te mete en el lecho;
roja franja de sangre, cuando bajo la lluvia
a torrentes su barro te vomitan los cerros.

Río hombre, pero hombre con pureza de río,
porque das tu azul alma cuando das tu azul beso.

Muy señor río mío. Río hombre. Unico hombre
que ha besado en mi alma al besar en mi cuerpo.

¡Río Grande de Loíza! . . . Río grande. Llanto grande.
El más grande de todos nuestros llantos isleños,
si no fuera más grande el que de mí se sale
por los ojos del alma para mi esclavo pueblo.

Desde el puente Martín Peña

Tierra rota. Se hace el día
el marco de la laguna.

Un ejército de casas
rompe la doble figura
de un cielo azul que abastece
a un mar tranquilo que arrulla.

Un ejército de casas
sobre el dolor se acurruca.

Hambre gorda corta el sueño
de enflaquecidas criaturas
que no supieron morirse
al tropezar con su cuna.

Río Grande de Loíza! . . . Blue. Dark. Red.
Blue mirror, fallen blue piece of sky;
naked white flesh turned black
each time night gets in your bed;
red stripe of blood when under rain
floods of mud vomit on the hills.

Man river, but man with purity of river,
because in your blue kiss you give your blue soul.

My very dear river. Man river. The only man
who, kissing my body, has kissed my soul.

Río Grande de Loíza! . . . Big river, big tear.
The biggest of all our insular tears,
if it were not for those flowing out
through the eyes of my soul for my enslaved people.

(Translated by María Arrillaga)

From the Bridge Martín Peña

Broken land. The day frames
the lagoon.

An army of houses
breaks the double image
of a blue sky satisfying
the lull of a tranquil ocean.

An army of houses
huddles over the pain.

Fat hunger cuts the sleep
of emaciated creatures
who did not know how to die
when they tripped over the cradle.

Marcha de anhelos partidos
pica la calma desnuda
donde recuesta su inercia
la adormecida laguna.

Una canción trepa el aire
sobre una cola de espuma.
Un verso escapa gritando
en un desliz de la luna.
Y ambos retornan heridos
por el desdén de la turba.

¡Canción descalza no vale!
¡Verso sufrido no gusta!
Tierra rota. Fuerza rota
de tanto cavar angustia.

Huesos vestidos alertas
a una esperanza caduca
que le hace mueca en las almas
y se le ríe en las arrugas.

Hacha del tiempo cortando
carne de siglos de ayuna.
Adentro la muerte manda.
Afuera el hambre murmura
una plegaria a los hombres
que al otro lado disfrutan
de anchos salarios restados
a hombres obreros que luchan.

¿Respuesta? —Brazos parados.
Sobra el mantel. No hay industrias.

¡Obreros! Picad el miedo.
Vuestra es la tierra desnuda.
Saltad el hambre y la muerte
por sobre la honda laguna,
y uníos a los campesinos,
y a los que en caña se anudan.

The march of departed desires
bites the naked calm
where the drowsy lagoon
rests its inertia.

A song climbs the air
on the tail of froth.
A screaming verse escapes
because of a slip of the moon
and both return wounded
by the disdain of the mob.

There is no value in a barefoot song!
A suffering verse has no acceptance!
Broken land. Broken strength
of so much digging anguish.

Clothed bones awaiting
a dying hope
that grimaces in their souls
and laughs from beneath its wrinkles.

The ax of time cuts
the flesh of hungry centuries.
Inside, death reigns.
Outside, hunger prays
to the men
who from the other side enjoy
fat salaries taken
from struggling workers.

Answer? Inactive arms.
The tablecloth is useless. The factories are still.

Workers! Bite your fear.
Yours is the naked land.
Jump past death and hunger
over the deep lagoon,
join hands with the peasants
and those who bend with the sugarcane.

¡Rómpanse un millón de puños
contra moral tan injusta!

¡Alzad, alzad vuestros brazos
como se alzaron en Rusia!

El rival de mi río

Yo te fui contemplando desde la carne al alma,
y me sentí culpable de un extraño delito
que me subía a los ojos en chispeantes miradas,
y se rompía en mi rostro en rubor infinito.

De pronto fue tornándose en pájaro mi boca,
y un sentimiento cósmico inundó mis sentidos;
me escondí en el secreto que estalló en tus pupilas,
y adiviné en tu rostro al rival de mi río.

¡Rio Grande de Loíza! . . . Alárgate en su vida.
¡Río Grande de Loíza! . . . Alárgate en su espíritu,
a ver si te descubres en la flor de su alma,
o en el sol de sus ojos te contemplas tú mismo.

El tiene en sus caricias el gesto de tu abrazo,
y en sus palabras cuelgan rumores parecidos
al lenguaje que llevas en tu boca de agua
desde el más quieto charco al más agreste risco.

Tú me besaste un día despertándome el alma;
él también me ha besado con un beso tan límpido,
que no sé allá en mi espíritu si posar extasiada
en el beso del hombre o en el beso del río.

¡Quién sabe si al vestirme con mi traje de carne,
y al sentirte enroscado a mi anhelo más íntimo,
surgiste a mi presencia en el río de sus ojos,
para entregarte, humano, y sentirte más
mío!

Let a million fists break
against such injustice!

Lift, lift your arms
as they were lifted in Russia!

(Translated by María Arrillaga)

My River's Rival

I went on contemplating you from the flesh to the soul
and felt the guilt of a strange crime
rising to my eyes in sparkling gazes
and breaking in my face in an infinite blush.

Suddenly my mouth began to change into a bird,
and a cosmic feeling overflowed my senses;
I hid in the secret that exploded from your pupils,
and I guessed in your face the rival of my river.

Río Grande de Loíza! . . . Extend yourself into his life.
Río Grande de Loíza! . . . Extend yourself into his spirit
to see if you discover yourself in the flower of his soul,
or in the sun of his eyes you contemplate yourself.

He bears the gesture of your embrace in his caresses,
and his words are hung with murmurs
as the language that you carry in your mouth of water
from the most tranquil pool to the most rugged cliff.

You kissed me one day, awakening my soul;
he has also kissed me with a kiss so clear,
I don't know deep in my spirit whether to lodge in ecstasy
in the kiss of the man or in the kiss of the river.

Who knows if putting on my dress of flesh,
and feeling you entwined to my most intimate longing,
you appeared to my presence in the river of his eyes,
to give yourself in human form, and to feel yourself more
mine!

¡Quién sabe si al bajarte del lomo de la tierra
para besarme toda en un loco delirio,
te humanizaste en su alma, y brotaste en corrientes
que una a una en mi tierra de emoción hizo nido!

¡Oh rival de mi río! . . . ¿De dónde me llegaste?
¿En algún país remoto te bañaste conmigo,
mientras en otra playa, con alguna doncella
se entregaba en amores mi voluptuoso río?

¿Me sorprendiste acaso en algún aguacero
violando claridades y callando suspiros,
portavoz ambulante de una raza de agua
que me subió a las venas en un beso del río?

¡Río Grande de Loiza! . . . Yo lo fui contemplando
desde la carne al alma: ese fue mi delito.
Un sentimiento cósmico estremeció mi vida,
y me llegó el amor . . . tu rival presentido.

El encuentro del hombre y el río

Recuerdo que los árboles recogieron sus sombras,
pálidos como sueños paralelos a mi alma.
Nubes recién bañadas se asomaron a verme
y un silencio de pájaros adornó mi llegada.

(Aparecía en el valle la luz de aquella niña
que venía por las tardes a seguir las quebradas.
La novia del Río Grande dibujaba a lo lejos
su rostro hecho de plumas y caricias de agua.

Volvía la amante suave, por los ojos del río,
la adolescente frágil que su cuerpo entregaba,
la que se fuera en noches a espiar las estrellas,
y que un día entre los hombres su vestido enredara.)

Who knows if in descending from the loin of the earth
to kiss me all over in an insane delirium,
you took human form in his soul and sprang in currents
that nested, one by one, in the land of my emotion.

Rival of my river! . . . Wherefrom did you come to me?
Have we bathed together in some remote country
while on another shore my voluptuous river
made love to some young maiden?

Did you surprise me perhaps in the rain
violating brightness and silencing sighs,
wandering spokesman of a race of water
that climbed up to my veins in a kiss of the river?

Río Grande de Loíza! . . . I went on contemplating him
from the flesh to the soul: that was my crime.
A cosmic sentiment shook my life
and love arrived . . . your foretold rival.

(Translated by María Arrillaga)

Encounter Between the Man and the River

I remember how the trees gathered their shadows,
pale like dreams parallel to my soul.
Clean clouds turned up to see me
and a silence of birds decorated my arrival.

(The light of that girl appeared in the valley,
she who would come in the afternoons to follow brooks.
The sweetheart of the Río Grande drawing in the distance,
her face made of feathers and caresses of water.

The soft lover returned, through the eyes of the river,
the frail adolescent surrendering her body,
she who at night would spy upon the stars
and who one day among men her dress would entangle.)

Mariposas que nunca levantaron el vuelo
fueron a dar al río la noticia anhelada.
Cuentan las margaritas que por breves momentos
la emoción de mirarme le detuvo las aguas.

(Desde aquel vago instante en que perdí su senda,
no levantó los ojos, ni enamoró más algas.
Me imaginaba siempre jugando en las orillas,
o dormida de amor, sobre su blanca espalda.)

Envuelta en el misterio de ser mujer o sueño,
yo caminaba a ciegas sobre mi propia alma.
De frente, mi amor loco por el río se encendía,
y a mi lado, mi amante, la emoción me inundaba.

Cuando perdí en mis pasos el impulso del río,
me le solté a la vida con voz desesperada,
y ya dura de golpes, sorprendí entre
mis años,
una mano que en luces mi dolor levantaba.

Yo le amé, por sus hondas incursiones celestes,
que callaron el hondo silencio de mi alma,
y noté que mis venas se poblaban de instintos
cada vez que sus brazos con mis brazos rozaban.

Su amor fue recogiendo los vírgenes paisajes
que al río, en su locura de amor, se le olvidaran;
y la humana corriente que saltó de su anhelo,
fue más ancha que el mar, y más fuerte que el agua.

Recuerdo que algún día yo le hablé de mi río,
y una como tormenta se agitó en sus entrañas.
No sé si fue mi pecho que tembló de recuerdo,
o si fueron mis ojos que asomaron nostalgias.

Me tomó de la mano como flor de misterio,
y siguió los guijarros que yo un día desandara.
Así fue que los valles recobraron inquietos,
la chiquilla silvestre del sendero de plata.

Butterflies that never flew before
went to give the river the longed-for news.
Daisies tell that for brief moments
the emotion of looking at me stopped his waters.

(From that vague instant when I lost his path,
he did not raise his eyes, nor wooed more algae.
He imagined me always playing on his banks,
or asleep in love, on his white shoulder.)

Wrapped in the mystery of being dream or woman,
I walked blindly, over my own soul.
In front, my mad love for the river would catch fire
and by my side, my lover, emotion flooding my being.

When I lost in my steps the impulse of the river,
I loosened up to life with anguished voice,
and already toughened by its blows, I discovered among
my years,
a hand that raised my pain in lights.

I loved him because of his deep celestial flights,
that soothed the deep silence of my soul,
and I noticed my veins become settled by instincts
each time that his arms brushed with my arms.

His love went gathering the virgin landscapes
that the river, in the frenzy of his love, had forgotten;
and the human current that sparked from his longing
was wider than the ocean, and stronger than the water.

I remember a day when I spoke of my river,
and something like a storm stirred in his being.
Was it my breast that trembled with the memory?
Was it nostalgia that showed through my eyes?

He took me by the hand like a mystery flower,
and followed the pebbles that I had left behind.
And so it was that the valleys anxiously recaptured
the wild child of the silver path.

Por un instante el alma se me fue de los pasos,
y me olvidé la vida, y me doblé las alas:
por entre las cortinas de extraviados relámpagos,
enteros de verdad, hombre y río se miraban . . .

¡Nunca tuvo más fuentes la bondad de mi amante!
¡La locura del río nunca tuvo más alma!
Los dos, claros de fuerza, se amaron en mi espíritu,
y besaron a un tiempo, mi emoción que lloraba.

Unos juncos morados que a mi lado dormían
recogieron el eco de unos labios de agua:
dicen lirios ingenuos que los juncos sensibles
nunca se despertaron por no herir la montaña.

(Tal vez en lo más íntimo del corazón
del río
presenciaron los lirios una muerte de alma . . .).

Poema para mi muerte

Ante un anhelo

Morir conmigo misma, abandonada y sola,
en la más densa roca de una isla desierta.
En el instante un ansia suprema de claveles,
y en el paisaje un trágico horizonte de piedra.

Mis ojos todos llenos de sepulcros de astro,
y mi pasión, tendida, agotada, dispersa.
Mis dedos como niños, viendo perder la nube
y mi razón poblada de sábanas inmensas.

Mis pálidos afectos retornando al silencio
—¡hasta el amor, hermano derretido en mi senda!—
Mi nombre destorciéndose, amarillo en las ramas,
y mis manos, crispándose para darme a las yerbas.

For an instant my soul left my steps,
and I forgot my life, and I folded my wings:
in between the curtains of lost lightning,
full of truth, man and river looked upon each other.

The kindness of my lover never had more fountains!
The frenzy of the river never had more soul!
Both, clear with strength, loved in my spirit,
and kissed at the same time, my emotion flowing.

Purple reeds sleeping at my side
picked up the echo of some lips of water:
the innocent lilies say that the sensitive reeds
never awakened so as not to hurt the mountain.

(Perhaps in the most intimate part of the heart
of the river
the lilies witnessed a death of a soul . . .)

(Translated by María Arrillaga)

Poem for My Death

Facing a wish

To die with myself, alone and abandoned
on the thickest rock of a deserted island.
At that instant a supreme longing for carnations,
and in the landscape a tragic horizon of stone.

My eyes filled with sepulchers of planets,
my passion spent, spread out, scattered.
My fingers like children watching a cloud losing itself
and my reason inhabited by immense sheets.

My pale affections returning to the silence
—even love, my brother, consumed in my path!—
My name untwisting, yellow in the branches,
and my hands clenching to give me to the grass.

Incorporarme el último, el integral minuto,
y ofrecerme a los campos con limpieza de estrella,
doblar luego la hoja de mi carne sencilla,
y bajar sin sonrisa, ni testigo a la
inercia.

Que nadie me profane la muerte con sollozos,
ni me arropen por siempre con inocente tierra;
que en el libre momento me dejen libremente
disponer de la única libertad del planeta.

¡Con qué fiera alegría conmenzarán mis huesos
a buscar ventanitas por la carne morena
y yo, dándome, dándome feroz y libremente
a la intemperie y sola rompiéndome cadenas!

¿Quién podrá detenerme con ensueños inútiles
cuando mi alma comience a cumplir su tarea,
haciendo de mis sueños un amasijo fértil
para el frágil gusano que tocará a mi puerta?

Cada vez más pequeña mi pequeñez rendida,
cada instante más grande y más simple la entrega;
mi pecho quizá ruede a iniciar un capullo,
acaso irán mis labios a nutrir azucenas.

¿Cómo habré de llamarme cuando sólo me quede
recordarme, en la roca de una isla desierta?
Un clavel interpuesto entre el viento y mi sombra,
hijo mío y de la muerte, me llamarán poeta.

To take the form of the last, the integral moment,
offering myself to the fields with cleanliness of stars,
later to bend the leaf of my simple flesh
and to go down without a smile, without a witness to the
inertia.

Let no one profane my death with their sobs
nor cover me forever with innocent earth;
let me in a free moment freely seize
the only liberty of this planet.

With what fierce happiness will my bones begin
to seek little windows in my dark flesh
and I, yielding, yielding freely and ferociously
to the open air and alone breaking my chains!

Who could detain me with useless dreams
when my soul begins to fulfill its task,
making of my dreams a fertile dough
for the fragile worm that will be knocking at my door?

Each time smaller my surrendered smallness,
each instant bigger and simpler the submission;
my breast might roll to initiate a bud,
perhaps my lips will nourish lilies.

What will my name be when all that is left
is my memory of myself on a rock of a deserted island?
A carnation placed between my shadow and the wind,
son of mine with death, they will call me poet.

(Translated by María Arrillaga)

Hugo Margenat (1933–1957)

Yo y Dios, hemos vuelto

Yo voy a disolver a Dios
en esta cerveza
para quitarle su amargura.
Para darle sabor
de disolución vasta de los cielos orientales.

Yo y Dios en líquido
fermentado, en la alegría
irrompible de las gracias
azules de sus vellos; en su cara roja de infinito

abriremos el círculo cerrado
para destornudar las siete maravillas
humanas de una carcajada.

Yo y Dios recitaremos versos
en la brega de Jayuya;
de la azada a la campana: más Lares.
Yo y Dios en las salinas calientes;
de las manos callosas: buena dureza.
En el brujo de una guayama:
más horas.
Ahora, por fin, en la noche del San Juan mío
recitaremos el último verso nocturno.

Yo y Dios, hemos vuelto a ti, con alas de madera.

Solamente una vez

Las vueltas del mundo.
Tus vueltas, mis vueltas.
Las vueltas de dos muñecos de pasta.

I and God, We Have Returned

I'm going to dissolve God
in this beer
to take away his bitterness.
To give him that taste
of vast disintegration of the oriental skies.

I and God in fermented
liquid, in the unbreakable
happiness of the blue
graces of his hair; in his red face of infinity

we will open the closed circle
to sneeze the seven human wonders in
one outburst of laughter.

I and God in the hot salt pits;
in the struggle of Jayuya;
from the hoe to the bell: and Lares.
I and God will recite poetry
of the calloused hands: good hardness.
In the sorcery of *guayama:*
and the hours.
Now, finally, in the night of the San Juan that is mine
we'll recite the last poem of the night.

I and God, we have returned to you with wooden wings.

(Translated by Digna Sánchez-Méndez)

Only Once

The world's turnings.
Your turnings, my turnings.
The turnings of two plastic dolls.

Has quebrado todas mis alegrías.
Has roto la uniformidad de la sonrisa
como poner un punto oscuro en mi diente.

En otro tiempo las cosas hubieran sido diferentes.
Tal vez tan opuestas como mi sombrero de luto a tus pequeñas manos.
Tal vez como un algo borrado, como un nudo fijo de ahorcado.

Ay, si te tuviera. Te he tenido.
Hoy me siento tan desolado
como ruinas enfriadas por la lejanía de una guerra.
En otro tiempo, en otro tiempo malvado
no hubiera podido esculpirte
porque mis manos estaban ciegas.

Unicamente me queda otro día.
Este día con sol, con caminos, con hierro, sin mar.
Me queda sólo el día y me lo jugaré con unos dados cargados.

La mano de hielo

Eran las tres de la madrugada cuando
apreté el cielo con una cuerda de guitarra.
No había tenido mucho espacio
para herirme y tuve que unirme
a lo incontable
y flagelarme con los dedos del llanto.

Recuerdo que la fiebre duró poco
porque tanto escupieron mi cara
que refrescaron mis labios agrietados.

Había llegado a esa hora
con mis manos rotas de sueños
y mi frente mojada de sales.

You have spoiled all my happiness.
You have broken all the uniformity of the smile
like putting a dark spot on my tooth.

In other time things would have been different.
Perhaps as opposed as my mourning hat to your small
hand.
Perhaps like something erased, like the tight knot of a
hanged man.

Oh, if I had you. I have had you.
Today I feel so desolate
like ruins cold from the remoteness of a war.
In other times, in other wicked times
I wouldn't have been able to sculpt you
because my hands were blind.

Only one day is left for me.
This day with sunlight, with paths, with iron, without sea.
I only have one day and I'll play it with loaded
dice.

(Translated by Digna Sánchez-Méndez)

The Ice Hand

It was three o'clock in the morning when
I pressed the sky with a guitar string.
I didn't have much space
to wound myself and I had to join
the infinite
and whip myself with the fingers of tears.

I remember that the fever didn't last long
because they spit on my face so much
that they refreshed my cracked lips.

I had come to that hour
with my hands broken by dreams
and my forehead wet from salts.

Había llegado con los ojos cortados de amor
hasta que al tocar su mano la mía
sentí en los interiores
hundirse un trópico en las bocas del ártico.

Septiembre

En septiembre vinieron días tan pálidos
como la frente de un enfermo.
Indescriptible.
Fueron días como árboles de pantanos,
penumbrosos, con miradas estiradas en la oscuridad.
Fue septiembre quien señaló
el fin
de los estallidos claros y azules.

Cuando se fueron las nubes
y el ensueño 810
más se amarró mi voluntad a ti.
Y tiraste de las amarras
con furia y desprecio
y no hubo consuelo
y rodaron los pétalos cortados
por las tijeras del bostezo.

Si el consuelo me hubiera
mirado fijamente a los ojos
el mundo se hubiera
quedado con muy pocas flores.

Es posible la muerte en las pestañas.
Al cerrar la ventana de cristal
no podrás ocultar mi camisa blanca
sobre el mar.
La goleta, el canal, el cielo
y yo
que me pierdo
todos los días de septiembre

Had come with eyes cut from love
so that even when her hand touched mine
I felt inside
a tropic collapse in the mouth of the arctic.

(Translated by Digna Sánchez-Méndez)

September

In September came some days
as pale as the forehead of a sick man.
Indescribable.
They were days like trees in the mire,
penumbras, with stares stretched in darkness.
It was September that pointed to
the end
of the clear and blue outburst.

When the clouds and
the 810 fantasy left
my will was tied more to you.
And you threw off the ties
with fury and disdain
and there was no consolation
and the petals fell cut
by the scissors of the yawn.

If comfort had looked
me directly in the eyes
the world would
have been left with very few flowers.

Death is possible in the eyelashes.
When closing the glass window
you can't hide my white shirt
over the sea.
The schooner, the canal, the sky
and I
who lose
all the days of September

en tus oídos.
No huyas de la vida de la muerte
en mi muerte de vida joven.

No huyas.

Sepa usted

Soldado: asesino de la patria.
Hombre, rechaza el uniforme que denigra.
Yo sé de miles de botas que se hunden
en la tierra nuestra, destrozándola.
Yo sé de la marinería borracha y sádica
que como una avalancha de blanco estiércol
se riega por calles y plazas vomitando
su negro sello de piratas.
Yo sé de los aviones que ametrallaron
nuestros tejados en un día de octubre.
Aquel horrible desprecio que llovía
en fuego sembrando olores profundos.
No olvides que la luz no pudo ser ocultada
y a su calor la patria suspiró transformándose
como un rojo beso en el abrazo azul y desnudo del aire.

Al frente

Rojo amigo,
iremos delante, en la primera fila,
para recibir con los ojos abiertos,
la primera lluvia de balas.
Y no caeremos,
iremos agónicos entre solas flores
viviendo la sublimidad
de la rosa
en la cruz del corazón.
Llevaremos la Palabra

in your ears.
Don't run from the life of death
in my death of young life.

Don't run.

(Translated by Digna Sánchez-Méndez)

You Should Know

Soldier: assassin of the nation.
Man, reject the uniform that degrades.
I know of thousands of boots that sink
into our land, destroying it.
I know of the sadistic and drunken sailors
who like an avalanche of white manure
spread down the streets and plazas vomiting
their black seal of pirates.
I know of the planes that machine-gunned
our rooftops one October day.
That horrible disdain that rained as
fire sowing profound odors.
Don't forget the light couldn't be hidden
and by its heat the nation sighed and was transformed
like a red kiss in the blue and naked embrace of the air.

(Translated by Digna Sánchez-Méndez)

At the Front

Red friend,
we will go ahead, in the first line,
to welcome with open eyes
the first storm of bullets.
And we won't fall.
We will go in agony between lone flowers
living the sublimity
of the rose
in the cross of the heart.
We will bring the Word

a las calles angustiadas.
Llevaremos el sol
en cada beso
como en cada verbo
una noche sublevada.
Romperemos la tristeza
como un canto de alegría
que va rompiendo la monotonía de un dolor.
Siglos con dolor de cadenas.
Ya no es posible seguir cayendo
sin levantarse,
es preciso caer
levantándose,
floridos de claveles,
mirando el polvo militante
que en la inmensidad
se fundó con el polvo de la sola estrella,
como un lirio desprendido
de nuestro mundo verde y abierto
acallado en múltiples cristales la muerte ausente.
Ya no es posible seguir cayendo
sin olvidar escribir sobre el pavimento
la sonrisa de un hombre amado.
Ya no es posible. . . .

Madera dura

Elías Beauchamp e Hiram Rosado
con un canto de ausubo
y una proclama de Bayoán
traen una bandera besada de calor eterno.

Vienen entre luces de sol inevitable
endureciendo el viento como azotes de tierra.
Entre campanarios y torreones
se acercan compaginando recuerdos,
levantando perdones, llevando
en los labios como una furia de rosa,
como un amor dulce de pitirres.

to the anguished streets.
We will carry the sun
in every kiss
as in every verb
a rebelled night.
We will break sorrow
as a joyful chant
that breaks the monotony of a pain.
Centuries with the pain of chains.
It's no longer possible to keep falling
without arising,
it's necessary to fall
arising,
blooming with carnations,
looking at the militant dust,
that in infinity
fuses with the dust of the lone star,
as a lily cut off
from our green and open world
hushed in multiple glass of absent death.
It's no longer possible to keep falling
without forgetting to write on the pavement
the smile of a loved man.
It's no longer possible. . . .

(Translated by Digna Sánchez-Méndez)

Hard Wood

Elías Beauchamp and Hiram Rosado
with a chant of *ausubo*
and a proclamation from Bayoán
bring a flag kissed by eternal heat.

They come between inevitable sunlights
hardening the wind like earth lashes.
Between belfries and towers
they approach collating memories,
raising pardons, bringing
in their lips like a rose fury
like a sweet love of kingbirds.

Elías Beauchamp e Hiram Rosado
traen el pulso y lo vienen propagando
en la noche del Yunque vigilante.
Las piedras calladas también vigilan.
Vigilan los astros, almas insomnes,
y las hojas ciegas de luna llena
hacen señales al camino desierto.

Elías y Rosado entre las lágrimas del río
ancho y subterráneo brotan en manantiales
como leche de madre rebelde cantando.
No es posible el olvido, quemantes suspiros
que esparcen terso perfume de gloria.
Llena el aire el zumo de vuestros corazones
que circula incorrupto por venas
de abierto amor sin llanto.
No es posible el olvido, olas de granito,
árboles infinitos, sal de la tierra.
No es posible porque estas noches
os he visto llenando el espacio
con la bandera del hombre indoamericano.

Eslabones

1

Estos son poemas para la Revolución.
Para leerse junto al fusil caliente
o tal vez durante el destierro o tal vez
durante la muerte.

2

Los niños harapientos, con madre o sin madre,
salen todos los días, como si fueran
una humanidad aparte, a pedir dinero
por las calles donde se anuncia
lo mejor que han traído los yankis.

Elías Beauchamp and Hiram Rosado
bring the pulse and are spreading it
in the night of the vigilant Yunque.
The quiet stones also guard.
The astros guard, insomniac souls,
and the leaves blind from the full moon
make signals to the deserted path.

Elías and Rosado among the tears of the wide
and underground river gush in springs
like milk from a rebel mother singing.
To forget is not possible, burning sighs
that disperse terse perfume of glory.
The air is filled by the sap of your hearts
that circulates uncorrupted through veins
of open love without an outcry.
To forget is not possible, granite waves,
infinite trees, salt of the earth.
It's not possible because these nights
you have seen space being filled
with the flag of the Indo-American man.

(Translated by Digna Sánchez-Méndez)

Links

1

These are poems for the Revolution.
To be read alongside a hot gun
or perhaps during exile or perhaps
during death.

2

The ragged children, with or without a mother,
go out every day, as if they were
a humanity apart, to ask for money
in the streets that advertise
the best that the Yankees have brought.

Hay un chico
que en paradas diferentes
va guagua tras guagua en busca de vellones.
Desde Martín Peña a Río Piedras
todas las mañanas
lo verán ustedes
con una cara de anciano
y una bandera de hambre.

3

Hay allá una casita, en el campo,
que se muere de miseria,
que se gasta de puro llanto.
Los muchachos trabajan otras tierras,
en el Norte.
Las muchachas lavan otras ropas,
en el Condado.

Ay la casita que se alimenta de barro,
que por él le viene la ira,
que por él vomita los gusanos,
que por él se endurecen las lágrimas,
que por él explotan las penas
y llega por fin la hora buena
en que se come a los norteamericanos.

4

Fue a pedir trabajo a un Banco.
Le dijeron que le avisarían por correo.
Pasaron los días como noches.
Era su cara larga y sus labios gruesos.
Sus labios eran más gruesos
mientras su cara se hacía más larga.
Era hueso. Volvió. Nada, esa era la palabra.
Todas las caras eran blancas.
Paco era negro.

5

Ramón   Eugenio   José
Pedro   Pedro   Pedro

There's one boy
who at different stops
goes bus by bus looking for nickels.
From Martín Peña to Río Piedras
every morning
you'll see him
with the face of an old man
and a flag of hunger.

3

There's a house, over there in the countryside,
that dies of misery,
that is worn out from pure weeping.
The boys work lands of others
up North.
The girls wash clothes of others
in the Condado.

Oh, the house that feeds on clay,
that through it comes the rage,
that through it vomits worms,
that through it the tears harden,
that through it burst the sorrows
and finally the right time arrives
in which it eats the North Americans.

4

He went to ask for a job in a Bank.
They said they would notify him through the mail.
The days passed like nights.
His face was long and his lips thick.
His lips were thicker
while his face became longer.
He was bones. He returned. Nothing, was the word.
All the faces were white.
Paco was black.

5

Ramón Eugenio José
Pedro Pedro Pedro

Tú no te irás.
Te quedarás siempre.
Tú no te irás.
Te quedarás en todo lo amado.
Tú no te irás.
Te quedarás en la tierra de la Vida.
Tú no te irás.
Te quedarás en mi silencio abierto.

6

Aquí estoy,
incansable como tu corazón,
abierto como las manos
simples y puras.

En las mañanas,
cuando distingo la luz bajo la cual
naciste,
escucho la voz recia de nuestra rebeldía de siglos.
En las tardes,
cuando escucho el rumorar de los árboles del camino,
veo tu abiertísima sonrisa blanca
y tu franco saludo y la fuerza
de la Patria y de la Fe ardiente
en tu frente ancha de luz
enriquecida por el dolor y el beso de la Inmortalidad.

No digamos más.

Maestro. ¡Tierra!
Aquí estoy
en nuevo brote de amor y vida.

Dios es bueno

Dios es un gato que nos mira.
De acuarela es su reino.

You won't go.
You'll always stay.
You won't go.
You'll stay in all that's loved.
You won't go.
You will stay in the earth of Life.
You won't go.
You'll stay in my open silence.

6

Here I am,
untired like your heart,
open like the hands
simple and pure.

In the mornings
when I distinguish the light under which you were
born,
I listen to the strong voice of our rebellion of centuries.
In the evenings,
when I listen to the murmur of the trees along the path,
I see your wide open white smile
and your frank greeting and the strength
of the Nation and of the ardent Faith
in your wide forehead of light
enriched by the pain and the kiss of Immortality.

Let's say no more.

Master. Land!
Here I am
a new spurt of love and life.

(Translated by Digna Sánchez-Méndez)

God is good

God is a cat that looks at us.
His Kingdom is of watercolors.

Es plomo a momentos,
de madera casi siempre
cuando boga sin sentido
por un río de azufre escarlata.

Cuando canta golpea al humo,
cierra las corrientes de éter
y le da rienda a los galopes
vestidos de harina solitaria.
Dios, señor de los espantos,
de los cadáveres y ricas elegías,
amamantador de sombras,
guardián indescifrable,
mudo adolescente de metáforas,
es quien ahoga el alma mía
en el aljibe de su boca
siniestramente inmensa
como un bostezo de planetas.

Dios es como yo, ateo,
duro, navegador insondable,
vagabundo de risas cortas
y miradas largamente estrepitosas.
Corta sábanas, trae carbón,
destruye paredes, levanta barricadas,
conmueve a la masa de pétalos,
llama a la revolución mundial
y entierra espinas de hambre cósmica.
Es anticapitalista, anticlerical y anti-imperialista.
Dios, izquierdista,
es el conspirador perpetuo.

Yo soy multitud

Multitud de bancos. Campanarios de San Agustín.
Son las seis en punto. Palomas en vuelo curvo.
Sueño a la media hora, a la media hora sueño
que ante los siete candelabros estoy sintiendo
la pasión del Loto Blanco crucificado.

At times he is lead,
almost always of wood
when he rows without thought
in a river of scarlet sulfur.

When he sings he strikes the smoke,
closes the currents of ether
and gives rein to gallops
dressed in solitary flour.
God, sir of dread,
of corpses and rich elegies,
suckler of the shadows,
undecipherable guardian,
mute adolescent of metaphors,
is the one who drowns my soul
in the cistern of his mouth
immensely sinister
like a yawn of planets.

God is like me, atheist,
hard, fathomless navigator,
vagabond of short smiles
and long deafening stares.
He cuts sheets, brings coal,
destroys walls, erects barricades,
moves the mass of petals,
calls the world revolution
and plunges thorns of cosmic hunger.
He is anticapitalist, anticlerical, and anti-imperialist.
God, leftist,
is the perpetual conspirator.

(Translated by Digna Sánchez-Méndez)

I Am Multitude

Multitude of benches. San Agustín's belfries.
It's six on the dot. Pigeons in curved flight.
I dream in the half-hour, in the half-hour I dream
that before the seven candelabra
I am feeling the passion of the crucified White Lotus.

No tendré el descanso de la lágrima de cera
en mi ser de vela alumbrado.
Golpetazo ha sentido el banco. Denuncia la presencia
mía en el inválido. La bóveda y los arcos.
Siento frío. Oremos . . .
Anoche cuando lo cerraron todo y la media noche
se abrió como una flor nunca negra, jamás blanca,
entré a caballo profanando.
Miré al jinete yo mismo mirándome desde el color
gastado
de la imagen retorcida de espanto y azote.
No supe advertirle que era también Silencio,
el padre alto, el que mira todo
desde un ojo profundo
de ave-marías y padre-nuestros.
Yo había venido desde los campos del Sur.
Veníamos como un segundo escondiendo la luna.
Las herraduras gastadas. Demasiado para proseguir
asaltando a los terribles sueños de la noche.
Soy yo el gran petrificado en sus ojos de fuego.
No supe que tenía nombre hasta que los mármoles
me nombraron por boca de la escalerilla
que va al púlpito. Allí estaba Padre Silencio
amarrando a los átomos porciones inmarcesibles
de su esencia de pan nuevo. Pan de vida.
Vida de hojas, existencia árbol,
lenguaje de las aguas planetarias, multimillionarias
vivencias,
voz del incienso que nos reúne
para él yo-soy-siempre tu cara y tus manos,
siempre la madera, el mármol, la cruz de metal
inseparable
Campanario de San Agustín.
Son las seis y media vuelta.
Las palomas regresan al reposo
de mi boca de salmo.
Yo soy la multitud
de sandalias
caminando.

Being like a lit candle I won't
have the rest of a wax tear.
The bench has felt a beating. It denounces my presence
in the invalid. The vaulted roofs of the arches.
I feel cold. Let's pray . . .
Last night when they closed everything and midnight
opened like flower never black, never white,
I entered, profaning, on horseback.
I looked at the horseman looking at myself from the faded
color
of the image twisted by dread and whipping.
I didn't know how to warn him that he was also Silence,
the holy father, the one who watches
everything from a deep eye
of Ave Marias and paternosters.
I had come from the countryside of the South.
We came like a second hiding the moon.
The worn-out horseshoes. Too much to keep
assaulting the terrible dreams of the night.
I am the great petrified one in his eyes of fire.
I didn't know I had a name until the marble
named me by the mouth of the small stairway
that goes to the pulpit. Father Silence was there
tying the atoms portions that can't be abridged
of his essence of new bread. Bread of life.
Life of leaves, tree existence,
language of the planetary waters, multimillionaire
living,
voice of the incense that reunites us
for him I-am-always your face and your hands,
always the wood, the marble, the cross of inseparable
metal.
San Agustín's belfry.
It's six and half turn.
The pigeons return to rest
on my mouth psalm.
I am the multitude
of walking
sandals.

(Translated by Digna Sánchez-Méndez)

Part Three

LATEST POETRY (from 1955)

José María Lima (b. 1934)

también en los ombligos acechan muertes . . .

también en los ombligos acechan muertes;
porque la muerte se aproxima en todas direcciones
con su carga inexorable de término.
en cada ojo hay un final durmiendo
y si a veces parece
que algún labio oscurece la tumba,
díganle al peregrino que se engaña:
que también hay espejismos,
que la nube revienta.
también en los ombligos hay espinas.
los abismos se escurren inadvertidos
hasta llegar de pronto
con su carga de tiempo envilecido
y nos golpea de súbito la cara
y repite las risas una a una
en sus paredes secas de caricias.
¡cuidado caminante!
ni tu mismo semblante
te acompaña cuando te sigue el dolor
empecinado en busca de tu tuétano.
ni siquiera tus huesos serán tuyos.
te quitarán los ojos cuando llegues,
y si acaso pensabas en tu garganta
es bueno que medites
—aún hay tiempo—
se escapará, será de otros
y quedarás silencio sobre arena,
pero arena perdida y sin espuma.
se reparten tu pelo en las esquinas,
tú lo sabes, y sin embargo, crees
que puedes alcanzar la orilla opuesta
con la única ayuda de tu caja
de ruidos especiales.

deaths lurk also in navels . . .

deaths lurk also in navels,
because death approaches from all sides
with its inexorable terminal load.
an end sleeps in every eye
and if sometimes it seems
that some lip obscures the tomb,
tell the pilgrim that he deceives himself;
that there are also mirages,
that the cloud bursts.
there are also thorns in navels.
abysms trickle out heedless
arriving suddenly
with their load of degraded time
and hits us suddenly in the face
and repeats the laughter one by one
in its walls dry of caresses.
beware traveler!
even your own countenance
won't accompany you when pain pursues you
stubbornly looking for your marrow.
even your bones will not be yours.
they will pull your eyes out when you arrive,
and if perhaps you thought about your throat
it might be good to meditate
—there is still time—
it will escape, it will belong to others
and you will remain silence on the sand,
but lost sand and without foam.
they portion out your hair in the corners,
you know it, yet, you believe
that you can reach the opposite shore
with only the help of your box
of special noises.

(Translated by María Arrillaga)

Los héroes

I

Siempre es más importante un hola bien dicho, porque hay gusanos atentos detrás de cada oreja. Los canarios se visten de gala y un inocente terror con cola de oro se pasea por las calles más humildes sin mirar hacia atrás. Es que llegó la moneda, llegó el embajador y llegó un pedazo de tiempo futuro (más de una gota) envuelto, a manera de crisálida, en sucia risa de marineros ebrios, para gloria de dueños, satisfacción de mercaderes y desgracia de tontos.

Ni siquiera suspiran las hormigas.

El insecto inocente guarda su melancolía como guarda también con cuidado sus alas. Siempre es posible caminar. A falta de cielo, suelo. Después de todo, dicen, es conveniente tener los pies sobre la tierra. ¿Y después? Más suelo. Proscribamos las alas. Adoremos el plano (horizontal por supuesto) ¡Tan sencillo, tan claro, tan limpio!

Sencillez, ésa es la palabra. Pero sencillez heroica y heroicidad sencilla. Sin heridas, sin sangre, sin angustia. Con muchas medallas y más monedas.

Conjuguemos:
Yo soy héroe
Tú eres héroe
El no es héroe
Nosotros somos héroes (O
estamos en camino de serlo)
Vosotros sois héroes
Ellos no son héroes

Porque él y ellos no existen. Solamente existimos, heroicos por supuesto, o próximos a serlo, yo, tú, nosotros y vosotros.

Pero ¡mirad! ¡No hay tumbas, ni lágrimas! Somos todos socios en la dulzura general, por fortuna hecha historia en un tipo de imprenta uniforme y sin mayúsculas.

¡Aplausos!
¡Albricias!
¡Eureka!

The Heroes

I

A well-said hello is always more important, because there are attentive worms behind each ear. The canaries dress up and an innocent terror with tail of gold walks on the humblest streets without looking back. It's that the coin has arrived, the ambassador has arrived, and a slice of future time has arrived (more than a drop) wrapped up, like a chrysalis, in dirty laughter of drunken sailors, to the glory of the owners, satisfaction of tradesmen, and misfortune of fools.

Not even the ants sigh.

The innocent insect takes care of its melancholy the same way it carefully takes care of its wings. One can always walk. When you lack sky, ground. After all, they say, it is convenient to have one's feet on the ground. And afterward? More ground. Let us outlaw the wings. Let us worship the plane (the horizontal, of course) So simple, so clear, so neat!

Simplicity, that is the word. But heroic simplicity and simple heroism. Without wounds, without blood, without anguish. With a lot of medals and more coins.

Let us conjugate:
I am a hero
You are a hero
He is not a hero
We are heroes (or are on our way
to becoming heroes)
You are heroes
They are not heroes

Because he and they do not exist. We only exist, heroically of course, or close to becoming, I, you, we and you.

But look! There are no tombs or tears! We are all partners in the general sweetness, made history by luck in a uniform printing type and without capitals.

Applause!
Good news!
Eureka!

¡Qué originales somos los
héroes gordos!

II

Convengamos en que "mañana" no existe. Sólo existe "hoy" y un poco (sin exageración) de "ayer." No nos mueve el egoismo personal a aceptar este supuesto. Sencillamente así resultan más sencillas las cosas y como hemos dicho, somos sencillistas.

Resumiendo:

"Hoy" se escribe con mayúscula.

"Mañana" no se escribe.

"Ayer" unas veces se escribe y otras no, dependiendo de las condiciones del tiempo y tomando en consideración las disposiciones contenidas en cierto horóscopo que nos ha sido confeccionado conforme a un poco de nuestra voluntad y toda la voluntad de los dioses y sus intermediarios.

Sea hecha la voluntad de los héroes y los dioses.

III

Una jaula de oro es una jaula, pero no hay que negar que es de oro. Es mal intencionado señalar lo primero sin detenerse a reflexionar sobre lo segundo y es sensato asegurar lo segundo.

¿Quién duda que el paraíso de las marionetas es el baúl (cerrado)? Exceptuando a Pinocho, y solamente por haber tenido la nariz demasiado larga.

Moraleja: Para baúles cómodos, narices cortas.

IV

¡A la carga! Los héroes al frente.
Pacatás, pacatás, pacatás.
El uniforme de los héroes todavía está limpio.
Pacatás, pacatás, pacatás.
Los héroes tienen ahora otro uniforme.
Pacatás, pacatás, pacatás.
¡Fácil!
Pero es extraño, ¿quién dijo ¡alto!?

How original we are
the fat heroes!

II

Let us agree that "tomorrow" does not exist. Only "today" exists and a little (without exaggeration) of "yesterday." We are not moved by personal egoism to accept this supposition. Simply, things seem more simple this way and as we said we like simplicity.

Summing up:

"Today" is capitalized.

"Tomorrow" is not written.

"Yesterday" is written sometimes and not others, depending on weather conditions and taking into consideration the dispositions contained in a certain horoscope manufactured for us in accord with some of our will and the full will of the gods and their intermediaries.

The will of the heroes and the gods be done.

III

A gold cage is a cage, but there is no denying that it is made of gold. It is ill-intentioned to point out the first without pausing to reflect on the second and it is sensible to affirm the second.

Who doubts that the paradise of the marionettes is the trunk (locked)? Excepting Pinocchio, and only because his nose was too long.

Moral: For comfortable trunks, short noses.

IV

Forward! Heroes to the front.
Clip, clop, clip, clop.
The uniform of the heroes is still clean.
Clip, clop, clip, clop.
The heroes now have another uniform.
Clip, clop, clip, clop.
Easy!
But it is strange, who said halt!?

(Translated by María Arrillaga)

Iris M. Zavala (b. 1936)

El gran mamut . . .

El gran mamut sueña quijotes
de enormes ojos de neón
monstruosa luciérnaga que enfoca
un continente desolado
o será una isla sola
protegida por el dios de los ejércitos
el que Moisés llevaba
y traía
humo viento fetiche
hágase la luz
ya hecha de metal
no usado por enormes
fábricas higiénicas lustrosas
donde un hombre o será un esclavo
amarillo negro y blanco
ya casi sin color
produce su artefacto
que en 1943 extermina
ángel de luz
satanás histórico
ya olvidado
que se reproduce y se transporta
en largos y admirables
retadores de sonido y tiempo
dirigidos por quijotes
vestidos de western
con cabellos largos
y pequeños mensajes
llama de amor viva
para Ho Twyn Li y Ernesto Pérez
carbonizados.

The Great Mammoth . . .

The great mammoth dreams quixotes
of enormous neon eyes
monstrous fireflies that focus
on a desolate continent
or is it a lone island
protected by the God of armies
the one Moses brought
and took back
smoke wind fetish
let there be light
already made of metal
not used by enormous
lustrous hygienic factories
where a man or is it a slave
yellow black and white
almost without color
produces his artifact
that in 1943 exterminates
angel of light
historical satans
already forgotten
who are reproduced and transported
in long and wonderful
challengers of sound and time
led by quixotes
in western dress
with long hair
and small messages
flame of living love
for Ho Twyn Li and Ernesto Pérez
charred.

(Translated by Digna Sánchez-Méndez)

Sonrisa mentira cohetes . . .

Sonrisa mentira cohetes
abre sus brazos de animal
acuático
o anaconda atrapado
el soldado
de Minnesota Filipinas San Juan
negro criollo all american
irracional
enorme gato amaestrado
que hunde sus uñas
perfumadas y sinuosas
en tibia carne
de otro hombre
voz incomprensible
en este mundo cuadriculado.

Smile Lie Rockets . . .

Smile lie rockets
opens his arms of an aquatic
animal
or a trapped anaconda
the soldier
from Minnesota Philippines San Juan
Black creole *all american*
irrational
enormous trained cat
that sinks his perfumed and
sensuous nails
into the warm flesh
of another man
incomprehensible voice
in this squared world.

(Translated by Digna Sánchez-Méndez)

Luis A. Rosario Quiles (b. 1936)

El juicio de Víctor Campolo
(fragmentos)

La calle:
—Una vez fuera de la escuela
caminaba setenta y seis, siete,
ocho, nueve, ochenta pasos
hasta la esquina del billar y el semáforo
donde endagaban los panas Cuco, Fele, Juan Pecho
y Nacho,
de nombre Ignacio "Sabor" Rodríguez,
conocido como "Sabor de Nacho."
Los panitas eran la muerte,
primero compartían el paraguas contigo,
te daban de lengua y te quemaban
con la salida cerrada y la burla rimada
y dicharachera.

La ganga:
"—No le tiren a este panita del otro caserío,
dice que no viene aquí por las mamis,
parece buena gentáin,
no le den tan duro que es buena gentáin,
aguántamelo que corre,
falto yo de pegarle un puñetazo
buena gentáin."

La chamaca:
"—Esta mañana estuve soñando con la novia,
estaban Arturo, Manuel y sus novias
y más nadie,
estábamos en casa de Ana, la de Manuel,
guillándonos bien chévere,
que Arturo le pegó a Irma

The Trial of Víctor Campolo
(fragments)

The street:
Once out of school
I used to walk seventy-six, seven,
eight, nine, eighty steps
to the corner with the pool hall and the traffic light
where the brothers Cuco, Fele, Juan Pecho
and Nacho,
by name Ignacio "Sabor" Rodríguez,
known as "Sabor de Nacho" hung out.
The brothers were too much,
first they shared with you their umbrellas,
they would get tight with you and then,
in rhymed mockery with no way out
full of heavy slang, they fucked your head.

The gang:
"Don't touch this brother from the other project,
he says he doesn't come here for the broads,
he looks alright,
don't bust him so hard he's OK,
hold him he's getting away
I still haven't hit him,
he's OK."

The chick:
"This morning I dreamt about my girl friend,
Arturo, Manuel and their girls were there
and no one else,
we were in Ana's house, Manuel's chick,
really making out,
Arturo hitting Irma

él se pasa dándole fuete,
y no había más nadie en la sala,
que estábamos besándolas,
y yo trataba de comerle el cerebro
con intención de algo más que besarla
y tocarle los senos,—Usted sabe ¿no?—
pero en ese momento desperté
y más nadie."

El baile:
"—Ojo, Man, está el oso que hace orilla
Man, aquel está bien buena, Man, y se mete adentro
Man, aquel títere no la suelta, ¡sea su madre!
Man, la de verde es fea pero tira y mide bien,
mete mano. Te digo: Feoca pero mete mano, Man,
Man, que es lo importante, ¡agua! ¡Man! ¡Agua!

La familia:
"—Digo que no sólo jode el calor
sino que menos aún se puede estudiar
con la televisión— ¡jodíos comerciales!—
Mi pai cantando la jodía canción de Daniel Santos,
mi hermano queriendo usar mi jodía camisa azul,
mi hermana porque trabaja se cree dueña.
Me gustaría que peleáramos menos, estar más unidos
como cuando Rafael tuvo el jodío accidente en Bayamón,
más unidos, mi Mai sufriría menos—"

La máquina de flipper:
"—Oh, bola, bolita plateada
que prendes las luces y haces los números
y los sonidos de las campanitas intermitentes,
y me permites quemar a Juan Pecho,
¡Oh Dios!, que la bola plateada toque
los círculos que guiñan con bombillos
de bastantes colores y sumen 10,
15, 25, 75, 125, no te acumules
por ese lado bola, 150, 160, avanza, enumera,
toma, toma, 185, 205, Juan Pecho ya casi
estás perdido, 230, ¡ahí! 280, 300.

he's always knocking her around,
and there was no one else in the living room,
and we were kissing them,
and I was trying to psyche her,
to do more than just kissing,
feeling her breasts, you dig?
but at this moment I woke up,
and no one else."

The party:
"Watch it, man, too many slicks around,
Man, that chick's into something, man, and she grinds,
Man, that cat doesn't let her go, motherfucker!
Man, the one in green is ugly but she moves well
gets down, I'm telling you: ugly but man she gets down,
Man, that's what matters; heavy! man! heavy!"

The family:
"I'm telling you it's not only the fucking heat
forget about studying
with the t.v., fucking commercials.
Pops singing that fucking Daniel Santos song,
my brother wanting to use my fucking blue shirt,
my sister thinks she's the boss 'cause she's working.
I wish we'd fight less, be more together
like when Rafael had the fucking accident in Bayamón,
more together, my mom would suffer less."

The pinball machine:
"Oh, ball, little silver ball
that turns on the lights and spaces out the numbers
and the sounds of the small bells,
and let me fuck up Juan Pecho,
Oh God, let the silver ball touch
the circles with blinking lights
with plenty of colors and total 10,
15, 25, 75, 125, don't crowd
on that side, ball, 150, 160, hurry
get it, get it, 185, 205, Juan Pecho you're almost
lost, 230, there! 280, 300.

Bolita de la cábala, hazme ganador,
325, no hay para nadie, bola plateada, numerosa,
bola rica, eres lo único que tengo, 400, 450,
lánzate, no, no, por ahí no, te vas a hundir,
Dios Mío, la bola se va a enterrar, no,
Dios Mío, si gano te prometo, no ¡Por Favor!
¡Qué hostia!

Little ball of fortune make me a winner,
325, no chance, silver ball, ball of numbers,
rich ball, you're all I got, 400, 450,
go, no, no, not there, you're going to sink,
Oh my God, the ball's going to go, no,
Oh my God, if I win I promise, no. Please!
Oh shit!"

(Translated by Digna Sánchez-Méndez)

Alfredo Matilla (b. 1937)

subway

del bronx el barrio la periferia convergen en
manhattan
down town la fábrica
mid town porteros ascensoristas lavaplatos
cocineros salen del subway otro túnel
a/desde la muerte un avión invertido un paso subterráneo
más abajo de la dispersión un hilo eléctrico en un hilo una
coyuntura de sabor de estómago
una reiteración de oscuridad y encierro suben
en racimos de los vomitorios ojos de sueño eterno como las
funerarias ojos enterrados en la tecata del token
salen andan van
a las factorías a joderse en el punto mecánico
del botón apretándose cadáveres catacúmbicos surgen
resortes
se disuelven se evaporan en ritmo pesado de sábanas
ahogadas
tren incrustado en el esófago corre
por las venas cura electrificada se ha
hecho pestañas carne huesos sangre
y la hermana brotada detenida bella esperando el fusil
bella que quiebre el subway tras los párpados
bella
que borre el sueño de rieles varicosos bella
¡DESPIERTA HERMANA!!!!

subway

from the bronx spanish harlem the periphery converge in
manhattan
factories down town
mid town porters elevator operators dishwashers
cooks come out of subways another tunnel
to/from death an inverted airplane a subterranean pass
further down from dispersion an electric thread by a
thread a meeting of heartburns
a reiteration of closeness and a darkness they come out
in bunches from the vomitories eyes of eternal sleep as
in the funeral homes eyes buried in the token's dope
they come up walk go
to the factories to be fucked up on the mechanical point
of the button huddled catacombical bodies spring
out
they dissolve evaporate with a heavy rhythm of drowned
sheets
train encrusted in the esophagus runs
through the veins electrified cure has
become eyelashes flesh bones blood
and a sister flowered-out still beautiful in wait for the gun
beautiful that shatters the subway behind eyelids
beautiful
that erases the varicose rails dream beautiful
WAKE UP SISTER! ! !

(Translated by Alfredo Matilla)

catálogo de locos—kimberna

kimberna por el boulevard con su vaivén felino su nariz
achatada
en s sus saltitos que lo delatan su mirada cuadriculada
la tarde es clara y dura el mar contra los zocos
de la perla
la luz salada clavando la isla
a cada martillazo el plás plás del agua
dos y media de la tarde kimberna negro baja por el
boulevard
kimberna gato san juan como un cromo pegado a la carne
hace tiempo
era kid bernard y boxeaba y tenía una claque que lo
seguía por los rings
y las sillas de tijera que lloró de alegría la noche de los
guantes dorados
en el sixto escobar la noche de kid bernard campeón fue
casi como
boxear en casa tan cerquita de la perla y cada ópercot
lo aproximaba más a kimberna los cocos secos y
las pesetas
después profesional peso mediano bailado hombreado
resortes mágicos de los bíceps la claque fiel
campeón cómo te sientes vaya man te sirvieron una
guachafita anoche
y así aduladores amigos de siempre de ya
de nunca
se sienta kimberna en la muralla de espaldas al mar
mirando pasar los
carros con pupilas telescópicas los brazos caídos
entre las piernas
como pencas muertas la noche anterior a la gran pelea
trató de reposar en la cama de esprines alta relajando los
músculos
mi man cuando llegues a nueva yol te quedas en casa
de mi cuñada
en el sauzs bronx la vellonera del bar guadalcanal a to
trapo y

catalogue of lunatics—kimberna

kimberna down the boulevard with his cat sway his nose
 flattened
in s his little jumps that reveal him his squared gaze
the afternoon is clear and hard the sea against the houses
 of *la perla*
the salty light nailing the island
at each hammer's blow the splash splash of the water
two-thirty in the afternoon kimberna black walks down
 the boulevard
kimberna cat san juan like a decal glued to the flesh a
 long time ago
he was kid bernard and boxed and he had a claque which
 followed him in the rings
and the collapsible chairs that cried with joy the
 night of the golden gloves
at the *sixto escobar* the night of kid bernard champion
 was almost like
boxing at home so close to *la perla* and each uppercut
brought home closer to kimberna the dry coconuts and
 the quarters
afterward professional middleweight danced shouldered
magic springs of his biceps the faithful claque
how do you feel champ dig man you had it made last
 night
and like that bootlickers old friends now friends
 never friends
kimberna sits on the wall with his back to the sea
 watching the
cars with telescopic pupils pass by arms fallen
 between the legs
like dead fronds the night before the fight
he tried to rest in the high bed with springs relaxing the
 muscles
man when you get to *nueva yol* you stay with my
 sister-in-law
in the *souse bronx* the jukebox in the guadalcanal bar
 screeching and

pelear en el mádison escuer garden haciendo esfuerzos
por no
registrar las palabras de puruco tú sabe la geba americana
no tiene
tanta pendejá hasta que se dio cuenta de que era tarde la
vellonera callada los perros alzaos la noche sólida de que
tenía que dormir y mañana me lo como un rascacielos de
mil pisos
un avión rodeándolo como un mosquito y el south bronx
era igual
a las urbanizaciones que empezaban a hacer
por hato rey
pero empinadas y que tenía que
y noqueó al sueño
iba a calcar la noche de los guantes dorados la
noche de kid bernard
campeón en hombros desde el sixto escobar
lo pensaban llegar hasta san juan
entrarlo por la plaza colón y luego
subirlobajarlo a la perla pero ya por el zoológico del
parque
muñoz rivera aunque seguían entusiasmados andaban
pensando que
mejor será dejarlo y después lo volvemos a agarrar cuando
lleguemos
y para el club de oficiales lo bajaron y lo abrazaban y le
dieron
palmaditas y a franqui que se daba la mota le cayó
la onda del pugilato e invitó al kid a cambiar unos
golpes en broma
al campeón se le olvidó que ya no lo cargaban
los adoquines de san juan fluyen hacia las alcantarillas
kimberna es una pantera de guarapo
las casas de san juan se vuelcan hacia adentro
kimberna nunca llegó al south bronx y al día siguiente
anduvo
rondando el guadalcanal cojiéndolo suave cambiando
impresiones con
sus fanáticos te lo vas a comer kid luciéndose con los
muchachitos

to fight in madison square garden trying hard
  not to
register puruco's words ya know american chicks
  aren't so
full of shit until he realized it was late the
jukebox silent the dogs talking back night solid that
he had to sleep and tomorrow i'll kick his ass a skyscraper
  of a thousand stories
a plane like a fly circling it and the south bronx
  was almost like
the urban developments that were starting to be built
  around hato rey
but standing up and that he had to
and he knocked out sleep
he was going to repeat the night of the golden gloves the
  night of kid bernard
champion carried on shoulders from the *sixto escobar*
they were thinking of taking him all the way to san juan
  of entering him through colon plaza and then
take him updown to *la perla* but around the zoo of muñoz
  rivera park
even though they were still enthused they were
  thinking that
it would be better not to carry him now and then we can
  pick him up later when we arrive
and by the officers' club they put him down and they
  were embracing him and they patted
him on the back and frankie who blew grass got into
a thing of fighting and invited kid to throw some
  punches with him for fun
the champion forgot they weren't carrying him
the cobblestones in san juan flow toward the sewers
kimberna is a cardboard panther
the houses in san juan turn outside in
kimberna never made it to the south bronx and the next
  day he
hung around the guadalcanal taking it easy
  small-talking with
his fans ya gonna finish him bragging to the
  young

cómo tú tiras un ópercot kid y él brincaba contestando
cuándo lo
vas a noquear tú crees que te dure dos rauns kid
pavoneándose
sus telescopios ciegos pinchan los carros la gente los
marinos
norteamericanos los turistas del fuerte san cristóbal el mar
detrás y abajo una mueca perdida en la nariz alfabeto de
kimberna
boulevard arriba se acercan tres muchachitos pipo lo llevó
en su
chevrolito al sixto escobar el escambrón palmas y cocos al
alcance
de sus puños las gebas dos emocionadas preludio del
escuer garden
uno de ellos lleva un coco seco en la mano los tres se
dirigen
a kimberna embobado en los puntos móviles de la calle
eje kimberna qué pasa panita ná aquí sentao
uno de los chamacos
juega con el coco lo tira al aire y recoge el rebote del
camerino
con olor a meao las paredes desconchadas allí se puso los
verdes
de raso esperó la hora en la camilla las manos vendadas las
últimas instrucciones del mániller el avión cuatrimotor los
músculos hablándole la negra del bronx en
español al principio
hasta que aprenda inglés no dejes que se te meta adentro
con la derecha
en el cadillac por el barrio trajeao
qué te pasa a ti
báilale juégale las piernas la ansiedad creciendo un
paquete
de edificios tuertos babeando escaleras de incendio
no te le tires
de lleno hasta el cuarto y el deseo tremendo de llegar al
ring tú tienes
molleros duros todavía pregunta uno de los pibes el del
pantalón corto

how do you throw an uppercut kid and he jumped as he answered when you are
going to k.o. him ya think he'll last two rounds kid showing off
his blind telescopes pinch the cars the people the american
marines tourists in fort san cristóbal the sea
behind and down there a lost grimace in the abc nose of kimberna
up the boulevard three youngbloods approach pipo took him in his
chevy to the *sixto escobar* the escambrón palm trees and coconuts at the reach
of his fists the broads two excited prelude for the square garden
one of them carries a dry coconut in one hand the three walk to
kimberna stupefied by the moving points of the street
hey kimberna what's happening brother nuttin just sitting one of the punks
plays with the coconut throws it up and from the air catches it on the rebound
the dressing room smelling of pee paint-chipped walls there he put on the satin greens
he waited for the time on the cot hands bandaged the
last instructions from his manager the four-engine plane
his muscles talking to him the chick in the bronx in spanish at first
until i learn english don't let him use
his right inside
in a cadillac through east harlem dresses cool
what do you think
dance around him use your legs anxiety increasing a bunch
of one-eyed buildings drooling fire escapes
don't go in
hard until the fourth and the great desire of getting to the ring do you still have
strong biceps asks one of the kids the one with the short pants

con carita de blanquito maricón kimberna flexiona los
músculos toquen les dice irguiéndose ellos han comenzado
el ritual
cuando bajó por entre las sillas de tijera sobre el jon del
diamante
de beísbol los amigos vitoreaban las mamis se guillaban y
cuando lo
anunció en esta esquina con pantalones el réferi la claque
chijí chijá
chijá ja ja pesando kimberna de san juan kimberna ra ra
ra kid bernard
y él llevó las manos juntas por encima de la cabeza y las
sacudió
todos tocan los bíceps y cómo tienes el estómago demanda
el gebito
trigueño y espigado él hace una tarzanada se golpea el
estómago de
tambor mira pallá qué duro el coco vuelve a saltar por el
ring metrónomo
tactac a la cara del otro tactac arriba kid dale duro el
vocerío
ahoga el yab del mar la caída de los cocos el rozar de las
pencas
sobre la sal del aire las risas gringas y nat king cole en el
officer's
club en el normandie y el escambrón los taxis las orquestas
del patio
tac tac tac el sol empuja el coco hacia abajo el nene lo
recibe
sonriendo y la cabeza kid la cabeza sigue tan dura apuesto
que no
el gordito espera los turistas oteando la perla desde el
fuerte
ahora kimberna se toca como a una puerta en la cabeza
toc toc los tres
se miran toc toc fuápiti el público alelado sorprendido
bocas abiertas
kid bernard comienza el descenso la caída desde el
rascacielos

with a little face like a rich faggot kimberna flexes his
muscles tough he tells them straightening himself up
they have begun the ritual
when he passed through the folding chairs behind home
plate in the
baseball diamond his friends cheered the broads dug him
and when the
referee in this corner announced him with green the
claque rah rah
rah weighing from san juan yelling kid bernard kimberna-
kimberna rah rah rah
and he saluted hands together over his head and he
shook them
they all touched his biceps and how strong is your
stomach demands
the tall and dark cat he does a tarzan he bangs his conga
stomach
wow man that's hard the coconut jumps again
by the ring metronome
clack-clack to the face of the other clack-clack
kill him kid the outcry
drowns the jab of the sea the fall of the coconuts
the friction of the fronds
over the salt of air the gringo laughs and nat king cole
in the officers'
club at the normandie and the escambrón taxis native
orchestras
clack clack clack the sun pushed the coconut down
cat gets it
smiling and your head kid your head is it as hard i
bet it isn't
the fatso waits tourists pry into *la perla* from the
fort
now kimberna knocks at his head
toc-toc the three
look at one another toc-toc-wham the public
surprised, amazed, open-mouthed
kid bernard starts the descent the fall from the
skyscraper

enredado en cuatro hélices la mueca repetida a cámara
lenta las
gotas de sangre volando fijas en los flash en los ojos
fanáticos
las tipas dos cerraron los párpados a tiempo la mascadura
suspendida
a la altura del hombro del réferi y en el ring el
movimiento
cayendo
separándose hacia su esquina
inclinándose con la mano derecha en alto
vuelven los gritos se reanuda el sueño pesado las hembras
dos
han bajado la cabeza plaf ha rebotado contra la lona la ha
manchado de
saliva sangre baba y el réferi uno dos tres y el otro en la
esquina
resoplando saltito va saltito viene y cuatro cinco seis
sueño granito
rascacielos enterrados en el mar que cañonea han callado
los fanáticos
se oye la gotera del cerebro siete ocho la mascadura
inmóvil
riéndose los ojos vidriados nueve la nariz cerrada diez toc
los muchachitos aprueban se empujan vacilan relajan
y el más callado
apuesto que no te puedes romper este coco seco en la
cabeza
avemaría y que no responde kimberna bueno hazlo sugiere
el trigueñito
en la chola por una peseta el otro le da el
coco kimberna lo levanta lo deja caer
lo rompe el agua le corre por la cara se ríe bobamente se
chupa
el agua que puede alcanzar se mete la cuara al bolsillo
y se
queda extraviado contra los turistas que fotografían hacia
abajo

entangled in four propellers the spasm repeated in slow
motion
blood drops flying fix in flashes in the eyes of the
fans
the broads two closed their lids on time the bite
suspended
at the height of the referee's shoulder and inside the ring
movement
falling
moving to his corner
bending with his right hand upraised
yelling again the heavy dream returns the broads
two
have lowered their heads plop has rebounded against the
canvas has stained it with
saliva blood drool and the referee one two three and the
other in the corner
a little jump here a little jump there and four five six
sleep granite
buried skyscrapers in the sea that cannons the fans are
silent
one hears the brains leak seven eight the immobile
bite
laughing glassy-eyed nine closed nose ten toc
the youngbloods approve push one another laugh groove
and the quietest
i bet you can't break this coconut on your
head
jesus of course answers kimberna o.k. do it suggests
the dark one
on your head for a quarter the other one hands him the
coconut kimberna raises it lets it fall
breaks it the water runs over his face he laughs stupidly
he sucks
the water he can reach puts the two-bits in his pocket
and he
remains lost against the tourists who look down from
their cameras

(Translated by Ellen G. Matilla)

Marina Arzola (b. 1939)

Cansancio
Muchacha de pies lindos

Pobres lacres de los pies . . .
de los niños seráficos cosidos.
¡Qué necedad de espanto en cada gruta!
Cuánto hay que recibirlo.
Si tu niñez nos diera cuatro pasos
y un beso reconstruido,
muchacha desdoblada por los besos,
llenada de clavitos.
¡Y hubiera un animal amedrentado
en cada leucocito!
¡Qué pasión de mis pies por tu cabeza!
¡Qué Tritón enardecido!
Correría diez pies, monzón,
un salto, de huevos ligeritos . . .
y llegaría a tu corazón tardo . . .
a reconstruirlo.
¡Ay, sí, mi amor: venado!
¡A reconstruirlo! . . .

San Petersburgo
(Antes de la Revolución de 1917)

Por las calles de este pequeño San Petersburgo
apoman los nidales de terrazas acústicas,
lacustres pececillos,
techos de calzas cuelgan en las calles,
techos de alambránicos trenes retorcidos,

Weariness
Girl of the Pretty Feet

Poor red sealing wax of the feet . . .
stitched by the seraphic children.
What foolishness of terror in each grotto!
How much one must receive it.
If your childhood gave us four steps
and a reconstructed kiss,
young girl unbent by the kisses,
full of little nails.
And if there was a frightened animal
in each leucocyte!
What passion of my feet for your head!
What a fiery Triton!
I would run ten feet, monsoon,
a leap, of light little eggs . . .
and would arrive to your late heart . . .
to reconstruct it.
Ah yes, my love: deer!
To reconstruct it!

(Translated by María Arrillaga)

St. Petersburg—
Before the Revolution of 1917

On the streets of this small St. Petersburg
like orchards the nests of acoustic terraces,
little lake fish,
roofs of breeches hang over the streets,
roofs of wiry trains twisted,

los restos de alpargatas estremecen
las tejas, los tejados alámbricos de zinc.

Un niño cuelga sus calzas calcetines
en la ventana azul del cementerio,
dormidero asustado del trajín cotidiano.
Un alma arrecia su ding dong
trebolado enclaustrado
tremecido por los hechos de cada día fiel.

Terrestres admoniciones cuelgan del
solamar de la ventana,
lacustres pececillos van y mecen
las ventanas azules del cerquillo
envuelto en madreselvas.

Azules amoníacos desprendidos
alcoholizan el cielo de las puestas:
azul, azul de fuego
hay en el mar ajado.
También una ventana.

Hay pequeños zorzales de palomas
acuáticas,
vencejos,
nidales de perdón y ruego al Padre.

Un pan anida en la oquedad rugosa
de los siglos:
junto al cercal aquel, a la dovela.

the remains of sandals shake the tiles,
the wiry roofs of zinc.

A boy hangs his breeches socks
on the blue window of the cemetery,
frightened sleeping place of daily hustle.
A soul increases its ding dong
cloistered clover patch
shook by the happenings of each faithful day.

Terrestrial admonitions hang from
the sunocean of the window,
little lake fish go and swing
the blue windows of the fence
draped in honeysuckle.

Blue ammonia unfastened
alcoholize the sky of the sets:
blue, blue of fire
there is in the wrinkled sea.
Also a window.

There are small thrushes of
aquatic doves,
martlets,
nests of forgiveness and prayers to the Father.

A bread nests in the furrowed cavity
of the centuries:
next to that fence, to the keystone.

(Translated by María Arrillaga)

Juan Sáez Burgos (b. 1943)

Cuento histórico en un solo idioma sin moraleja

Primera Parte

Había una vez
y dos son tres
y todavía es,
  un pedazo pequeño de la tierra
en medio de la mar:
  aquel pedazo se llenó de indios
desnudos como el bronce bajo el sol.
Pasaron vientos y pasaron olas
y llegaron en barcos unos blancos, y indios de
    bronce
bajo el sol
  lucharon y lucharon y murieron, y los blancos de barbas
bajo el sol
  mataron y mataron y vencieron.
Viva la Cruz y Viva el rey
  llenos de sangre porque así es la ley!
De una tierra más grande y más poblada se trajeron los
    blancos unos negros
desnudos de caoba bajo el sol. Les pusieron cadenas, los
    marcaron,
les hicieron beberse su sudor.
Por el Rey y por la Cruz llenos de odio rezan
    a Jesús.

Segunda Parte

Había una vez
y dos son tres
y todavía es,
  aquel mismo pedazo de la tierra

Historic Tale in One Language Without a Moral

Part I

Once upon a time
and twice are three
and still is,
  a small piece of the earth
in the middle of the sea:
  that piece was filled with Indians
naked like bronze under the sun.
Winds passed and waves passed
and in boats some whites arrived, and the Indians of
    bronze
under the sun
  fought and fought and died, and the whites with beards
under the sun
  killed and killed and conquered.
Long live the Cross and long live the King
  full of blood because that is the law!
From a larger, more peopled land, the whites brought
    some blacks
naked, mahogany under the sun. They chained them,
    they branded them,
they made them drink their sweat.
For the King and for the Cross filled with hate they pray
    to Jesus.

Part II

Once upon a time
and twice are three
and still is,
  that same piece of earth

en medio de la mar;
aquel pedazo lleno está de gente
vestidos y mezclados bajo el sol.
Pasaron luchas y pasaron guerras
y llegaron en buques unos rubios, y criollos vestidos
bajo el sol
lucharon y lucharon; se rindieron, y los rubios
rosados
bajo el sol mataron y mataron se rieron.
Viva Wall Street y Santa Claus "and obey bastards this is
the law."
De su tierra más grande y más poblada se trajeron los
rubios unas bases
llenititas de bombas bajo el sol; les pusieron soldados y
cañones
e hicieron todo esto por su "sport."
Por Santa Claus y Wall Street marchan hacia la guerra
"dirty spiks."

Había una vez
y dos son tres
y todavía es . . .

Deliberadamente

Deliberadamente
me he propuesto vivir,
con toda la intención lo estoy haciendo
y pido una sonrisa por el gesto.

Una pequeña
musiquita idiota
me rodea,
un sol de atardecer
prosaico y feo
atraviesa un cristal donde me encuentro.

in the middle of the sea;
that piece is filled with people
dressed and mixed under the sun.
Struggles passed and wars passed
and some blonds arrived in warships, and creoles dressed under the sun
fought and fought; they surrendered, and the pink blonds
under the sun killed and killed; they laughed.
Long live Wall Street and Santa Claus "*and obey bastards this is the law*"
From their larger, more peopled land the blonds brought some bases
full full full with bombs under the sun; they put there soldiers and cannons
and they did all this for "*sport.*"
For Santa Claus and for Wall Street "*dirty spiks*" march off to war.

Once upon a time
and twice are three
and still is . . .

(Translated by Ellen G. Matilla)

Deliberately

Deliberately
I have resolved to live,
I am doing it with all of my intention
and I ask for a smile for the gesture.

A small
idiotic little music
surrounds me,
a setting sun
prosaic and ugly
penetrates a glass where I find myself.

Se le puede cantar a la belleza,
uno la lleva
    o no la lleva adentro,
yo por lo pronto traje conmigo un poco,
(por si acaso)
pero pienso guardarla para luego.

    El que se quede
serio ahora,
el que no estalle en risas como un cerdo,
el que no sepa que las rosas muerden,
y ésta es una comedia,
un cuento que me invento para pasar el tiempo
sin ninguna intención, sin decir nada
y sin ponerme a revivir recuerdos: ése
que se levante,
    cierre el puño,
piense entre su camisa lo que siente,
y ponga a caminar sus dos zapatos.

One can sing to beauty,
one carries it
  or does not carry it within,
I for the time being brought some with me
(just in case)
but I intend to save it for later.

  He who remains
serious now,
he who does not burst into laughter like a pig,
he who does not know that roses bite,
and this is a comedy,
a story I am inventing to while away the time
without any intention, without saying anything
and without reviving memories:
let him stand,
  close his fist,
think between his shirt what he feels,
and put his two shoes to walk.

(Translated by María Arrillaga)

Pedro Pietro (b. 1944)

The Broken English Dream

I

....
....
....
....

....
....
....
....

....
....
....
....

....
....
....
....

II

,,,,,,,,,,,,,,,,,,,,,,
,,,,,,,,,,,,,,,,,,
,,,,,,,,,,,,,,,,,,,,,,
,,,,,,,,,,,,,,,,,,

,,,,,,,,,,,,,,,,,,,,,,
,,,,,,,,,,,,,,,,,,
,,,,,,,,,,,,,,,,,,,,,,
,,,,,,,,,,,,,,,,,,

Sueño en inglés goleta

I

....
.........!!......!
....
.........!!......!

....
.........!!......!
....
.........!!......!

!......!!.........
....
!......!!.........
....

!......!!.........
....
!......!!.........
....

(Traducción: Alfredo Matilla)

II

,,,,,,,,,,,,,,,,,,,,,,
,,,,,,,,,,,,,,,,,,
,,,,,,,,,,,,,,,,,,,,,,
::::::::::::::::::

,,,,,,,,,,,,,,,,,,,,,,
,,,,, ,,,,,,,,,,,
,,,,,,,,, ,,,,,,, ,,
,,,,,,,,,,,,,,,,,,

,,,,,,,,,,,,,,,,,,,,,,
,,,,,,,,,,,,,,,,,,,
,,,,,,,,,,,,,,,,,,,,,,
,,,,,,,,,,,,,,,,,,

,,,,,,,,,,,,,,,,,,
,,,,,,,,,,,,,,,,,,,,,,
,,,,,,,,,,,,,,,,,,
,,,,,,,,,,,,,,,,,,,,,,

III

....
,,,,,,,,,,,,,,,,,,,,,,
....
,,,,,,,,,,,,,,,,,,,,,,

....
,,,,,,,,,,,,,,,,,,,,,,
....
,,,,,,,,,,,,,,,,,,,,,,

....
,,,,,,,,,,,,,,,,,,,,,,
....
,,,,,,,,,,,,,,,,,,,,,,

....
,,,,,,,,,,,,,,,,,,,,,,
....
,,,,,,,,,,,,,,,,,,,,,,

IV

;;;;;;;;;;;;;;;;;;;;;;
;;;;;;;;;;;;;;;;;;
;;;;;;;;;;;;;;;;;;;;;;
;;;;;;;;;;;;;;;;;;

,,,,,,,,,,,,,,,,,,,,,,,
,,,,,,,,,,,,,,,,,,,
,,,,,,,,,,,,,,,,,,,, ,
,, ,,,,,,,,,,,,,,,

,,,,,,,,,,,,,,,,,,,,,,,
,,,,,,,,,,,,,,,,,,,
,,,,,,,,,,,,,,,,,,,,,,,
:

(Traducción: Ellen G. Matilla)

III

....
,,,,,,,,,,,,,,,,,,,,,,,
....
,,,,,,,,,,,,,,,,,,,,,,,

;;;;;;;;;;;;;;;;;;;
,,,,,,,,,,,,,,,,,,,,,,,
....
;;;;;;;;;;;;;;;;;;;;;;;

....
,,,,,,,,,,,,,,,,,,,,,,,
....
,,,,,,,,,,,,,,,,,,,,,,,

;;;;;;;;;;;;;;;;;;;
,,,,,,,,,,,,,,,,,,,,,,,
....
;;;;;;;;;;;;;;;;;;;;;;;

(Traducción: Alfredo Matilla)

IV

;;;;;;;;;;;;;;;;;;;;;;;;;;
;;;;;;;;;;
;;;;;;;;;;;;;;;;;;
;;;;;;;;;;;;;;

;;;;;;;;;;;;;;;;;;

;;;;;;;;;;;;;;;;;;;;;;;

;;;;;;;;;;;;;;;;;;

;;;;;;;;;;;;;;;;;;;;;;;

;;;;;;;;;;;;;;;;;;

;;;;;;;;;;;;;;;;;;;;;;;

;;;;;;;;;;;;;;;;;;

;;;;;;;;;;;;;;;;;;;;;;;

;;;;;;;;;;;;;;;;;;;;;;;

;;;;;;;;;;;;;;;;;;

;;;;;;;;;;;;;;;;;;;;;;;

;;;;;;;;;;;;;;;;;;

V

??????????????????????

; ; ; ; ; ; ; ; ; ; ; ; ; ; ; ; ; ;

; ; ; ; ; ; ; ; ; ; ; ; ; ; ; ; ; ;
??????????????????????

;;;;;;;;;;;;;;;;;;;;;;
??????????????????
??????????????????

;;;;;;;;;;;;;;;;;;;;;;

??????????????????????

;;;;;;;;;;;;;;;;;;

;;;;;;;;;;;;;;;;;;
??????????????????????

;;;;;;;;;;;;;;;;;;;;;;
??????????????????
??????????????????

;;;;;;;;;;;;;;;;;;;;;;

;;;

;;;;;;;;;;;;;;;;;;;;;;;;;;;;;;;

;;;;;;;;;;;;;;;;

;;;;;;;;;;;;;;;;;;;

;;;;;;

;;;;;;;;;;;;;;;;;;;;;;;;;;

;;;;;;;;;;

;;;;;;;;;;;;;;;;;;;;;

;;;;;;;;;;;;;;;;;;;;;;;;;;;

;;;;;;;;;;

;;;;;;;;;;;;;;;;;;;;

;;;;;   .

(Traducción: Alfredo Matilla)

V

¿¿¿¿¿¿¿¿¿¿¿¿¿¿¿¿¿¿¿¿¿¿
; ; ; ; ; ; ; ; ; ; ; ; ; ; ; ; ; ;
; ; ; ; ; ; ; ; ; ; ; ; ; ; ; ; ; ;
??????????????????????

;;;;;;;;;;;;;;;;;;;;;;
¿¿¿¿¿¿¿¿¿¿¿¿¿¿¿¿¿¿
??????????????????

;;;;;;;;;;;;;;;;;;;;;;

¿¿¿¿¿¿¿¿¿¿¿¿¿¿¿¿¿¿¿¿¿¿
; ; ; ; ; ; ; ; ; ; ; ; ; ; ; ; ; ;
; ; ; ; ; ; ; ; ; ; ; ; ; ; ; ; ; ;
??????????????????????

;;;;;;;;;;;;;;;;;;;;;;
¿¿¿¿¿¿¿¿¿¿¿¿¿¿¿¿¿¿
??????????????????

;;;;;;;;;;;;;;;;;;;;;;

(Traducción: Alfredo Matilla)

VI

??????????????????????
??????????????????
??????????????????????
??????????????????

??????????????????
??????????????????????
??????????????????
??????????????????????

??????????????????????
??????????????????
??????????????????????
??????????????????

??????????????????
??????????????????????
??????????????????
??????????????????????

VI

⸘⸘⸘⸘⸘⸘⸘⸘⸘⸘⸘⸘⸘⸘⸘⸘⸘⸘⸘⸘⸘⸘
⸘⸘⸘⸘⸘⸘⸘⸘⸘⸘⸘⸘⸘⸘⸘⸘⸘⸘
⸘⸘⸘⸘⸘⸘⸘⸘⸘⸘⸘⸘⸘⸘⸘⸘⸘⸘⸘⸘⸘⸘
⸘⸘⸘⸘⸘⸘⸘⸘⸘⸘⸘⸘⸘⸘⸘⸘⸘⸘

⸘⸘⸘⸘⸘⸘⸘⸘⸘⸘⸘⸘⸘⸘⸘⸘⸘⸘⸘⸘⸘⸘
⸘⸘⸘⸘⸘⸘⸘⸘⸘⸘⸘⸘⸘⸘⸘⸘⸘⸘
⸘⸘⸘⸘⸘⸘⸘⸘⸘⸘⸘⸘⸘⸘⸘⸘⸘⸘⸘⸘⸘⸘
⸘⸘⸘⸘⸘⸘⸘⸘⸘⸘⸘⸘⸘⸘⸘⸘⸘⸘

⸘⸘⸘⸘⸘⸘⸘⸘⸘⸘⸘⸘⸘⸘⸘⸘⸘⸘⸘⸘⸘⸘
⸘⸘⸘⸘⸘⸘⸘⸘⸘⸘⸘⸘⸘⸘⸘⸘⸘⸘
⸘⸘⸘⸘⸘⸘⸘⸘⸘⸘⸘⸘⸘⸘⸘⸘⸘⸘⸘⸘⸘⸘
⸘⸘⸘⸘⸘⸘⸘⸘⸘⸘⸘⸘⸘⸘⸘⸘⸘⸘

⸘⸘⸘⸘⸘⸘⸘⸘⸘⸘⸘⸘⸘⸘⸘⸘⸘⸘⸘⸘⸘⸘
⸘⸘⸘⸘⸘⸘⸘⸘⸘⸘⸘⸘⸘⸘⸘⸘⸘⸘
⸘⸘⸘⸘⸘⸘⸘⸘⸘⸘⸘⸘⸘⸘⸘⸘⸘⸘⸘⸘⸘⸘
⸘⸘⸘⸘⸘⸘⸘⸘⸘⸘⸘⸘⸘⸘⸘⸘⸘⸘

(Traducción: Alfredo Matilla)

Jorge María Ruscalleda Bercedóniz (b. 1944)

Consejo

Escúchame, amigo mío: te lo dije una noche
en casa de mi padre.
Te lo dije serenamente después de haberte dado
algunos tragos.
(Y tú bien sabes que aún no había tomado,
no porque sea un abstemio ni nada parecido,
sino, sencillamente, porque estaba en la casa
de mi padre.)

Te dije pausadamente cómo a mí me joroba
que me vengan con cuentos,
de esos cuentos, tú sabes,
que no valen un bledo.
Es decir, que si tengo en perspectiva
una beca de tres años
(tenía, debo decir ahora),
para estudiar un doctorado.
Pero, claro, eso ya a nadie importa.

Lo que te había dicho escuetamente
es que no me interesa
que tú vengas
a hablarme de los votos que valen dos cincuenta
(que, para los efectos, es lo mismo
si costaran un millón y medio).

Lo que sucede realmente
es que mi amigo Papo se siente muy enfermo,
(mi gran amigo Papo, que es mucho más que todo
esto) . . .
. . . Y en medio de los votos, del trabajo,
los lujos; en medio del estudio,
de tantas recomendaciones;

Advice

Listen, my friend: I told you one evening
in my father's house.
I told you calmly after having given you
a few drinks.
(And you know very well that I hadn't drunk,
not because I abstain or anything like that,
but, simply, because I was in
my father's house.)

I told you slowly since it annoys me
that people tell me tall tales,
you know, those tales,
that aren't worth a damn.
I mean, I am looking forward to
a three-year scholarship
(I was, I should say now),
to study for a doctorate.
But, of course, that doesn't matter to anyone, anymore.

What I had simply told you
is that it doesn't interest me
that you come and
tell me of the votes that cost two fifty
(which in the long run, is the same
as if they cost a million and a half).

What's really happening
is that my friend Papo feels very sick,
(my good friend Papo, who is much more than all of
this) . . .
. . . And in the midst of all the votes, the work,
the luxuries, in the midst of the studying,
of so many recommendations,

en medio de los títulos que exigen
más que ninguna cosa . . . En fin,
de las aspiraciones íntimas
y las claudicaciones,
yo te puedo decir que lo mejor será olvidarnos
de esas pequeñas situaciones
y poner atención a aquellas circunstancias
inevitablemente serias:
Como el caso de Papo, por ejemplo;
la entrega de las minas,
la venta de la Patria,
y el traqueteo audaz de los políticos de oficio
que nos quieren llevar al matadero . . .
Y sobre todo, que fijes la atención
sobre los hombres pobres, que pasan hambre
veinticuatro horas al día, que se rompen el lomo
trabajando hasta dejar el bofe,
para que aquellos que ahora mismo
te han puesto en tres y dos,
se pasen las semanas, los meses y los años,
haciéndoles el cuento a los ingenuos como tú,
en los bancos de las plazas.

Amigo mío, olvida esos fulanos
que te vienen a hablar de Socialismo,
y viven como reyes y tienen
ciento ochenta mil y pico de dólares
guardados en un banco.
No dejes que te tienten,
ellos conocen tu origen,
y saben las penurias que pasaste
para alcanzar el ruin Bachillerato.

No hagas caso, aunque te juren
que creen en la Justicia Social;
que creen en la Independencia, pero que son de los callados;
cuando tú sabes que en verdad
no fueron nunca ni siquiera patriotas de borrachera,
o los que ahora sobran: mártires de verano.

Vuelve al Pueblo, a los obreros curtidos

in the midst of the titles that require
more than anything else . . . Finally,
of those intimate aspirations
and falterings;
I can tell you that it's better to forget
those petty situations
and pay attention to those
inevitably serious circumstances:
Like Papo's case for example;
the surrender of the mines,
the selling out of the Fatherland,
the bold shuffling by the professional politicians
who want to take us to the slaughterhouse . . .
More than anything, fix your attention
on poor men, who starve
twenty-four hours a day, who break their backs
working until panting,
so that those who now have you
neither here nor there,
pass the weeks, the months and the years,
telling tall tales to innocents like you,
on the benches in the plaza.

My friend, forget those so and so's
who come to talk about Socialism,
and live like kings and have
over one hundred thousand dollars
kept in a bank.
Don't let them tempt you,
they know your background,
and know the penuries you went through
to get your worthless B.A.

Don't pay attention, even if they swear
that they believe in social justice:
that they believe in independence, but are of the silent
ones;
when you know in fact
that they were never even patriots of drunkenness,
or those that there are too many of: summer martyrs.

Return to the people, to the tan workers

de tu barrio; háblales del sufrimiento,
del valor;
explícales lo fácil que es sentirse alguna vez tentado
por las cosas ligeras, por las novias, el carro,
las urbanizaciones y los amigos que no les interesa nada.
Ellos comprenderán a fondo qué les dices.

Y para terminar esto de una vez, recuerda
que de nada vale el carro, la casa, la novia,
la familia y la Patria,
si a un hombre le sucede
—como dijo don Pedro—, que empieza a resbalar
y ya no para hasta romperse el pescuezo.

Que no digan los poetas . . .

A Billy Cajigas
y a Carmelo Rodríguez Torres

Que no digan los poetas
que le están cantando
a la arena, a los caracoles, a las olas,
a la espuma, al mar y al pleamar,
que no estamos diciendo la canción.

Que no digan los poetas
en éxtasis con Dios,
y con la Virgen y los santos y el cielo,
y el misterio y la eternidad,
que no estamos gritando la canción.

Que no digan los poetas
del alba o el rosicler,
de las flores, la piña, la abeja, las hojas,
la china, la miel, los nísperos, el polen,
los árboles, la oruga, el capullo, la crisálida, la mariposa,
el ruiseñor, la alondra, las palomas, las garzas,
la golondrina,
el invierno, la primavera, el verano, el otoño,
que no estamos mordiendo la canción.

of your neighborhood; speak to them of suffering,
  of courage;
explain to them how you can easily be tempted sometimes
by superficial things, by sweethearts, the car,
the houses and those friends who are interested in nothing
In substance they'll understand what you tell them.

And to finish this once and for all, remember
that the car, the house, the sweetheart,
the family, and the fatherland are worth nothing,
  if it happens that a man
—as Don Pedro said—begins to slip
and can't stop until he breaks his neck.

(Translated by Digna Sánchez-Méndez)

Poets Shouldn't Say . . .

To Billy Cajigas
and Carmelo Rodríguez Torres

Poets shouldn't say
that they are singing
to the sand, to the snails, to the waves,
to the froth, to the sea, and to the palm grove,
and that we aren't saying the song.

Poets shouldn't say
in ecstasy with God,
and with the virgin, and the saints and heaven,
and the mystery and eternity,
that we aren't yelling the song.

Poets shouldn't say
of the dawn or of the roseate,
of the flowers, the pineapple, the bee, the leaves,
the orange, the honey, the medlars, the pollen,
the trees, the caterpillar, the bud, the chrysalis,
the butterfly, the nightingale, the lark, the pigeons,
  the herons, the swallow
the winter, the spring, the summer, the autumn,
that we aren't biting the song.

Que no digan los poetas del Yo íntimo,
sentados frente a las aguas de Narciso,
o en las faldas de la amada,
sea de carne o sea de espíritu,
que no estamos muriendo la canción.

Porque, sepan ustedes,
que nosotros sabemos la canción.
Esa canción oscura de las noches del hambre y del frío,
esa canción amarga de los días sin leche ni pan,
esa canción horrible de los cuerpos sin telas ni abrigos,
esa canción nefasta de la intemperie
—sol y sereno—desde que nace el día
hasta que muere la vida tendida
en la sección misérrima de un hospital.

Porque, sepan ustedes,
nosotros sabemos en verdad que este pueblo pasa hambre.
Porque hemos oído y hemos visto,
con estos ojos que se los ha de tragar la tierra,
a una madre pidiendo media libra de arroz,
media de habichuelas y una cola de bacalao,
o media libra de fideos
y dos onzas de jamón.

Y eso no es todo.
Hemos visto a los niños con guarapitos,
desde el primer grito hasta que el padre llega sucio de las cañas,
o la madre de alguna fábrica de bolas.
O, por el contrario, durante el tiempo muerto,
al padre chiripiando,
y la madre . . . la madre está . . . viviendo.

Que no digan los señores poetas de los sonetos y las décimas,
de la diafanidad, de los certámenes y de las academias,
que esto es sencillamente tremendismo de la juventud.
¡Que no digan los señores señorones, poetísimos,
que no estamos llorando la canción!

Poets shouldn't speak of the inner I,
sitting before the waters of Narcissus,
or in the lover's lap,
be it of flesh, or be it of spirit
that we aren't dying the song.

Because you should know,
that we know the song.
That dark song of the nights of hunger and cold,
that bitter song of the days without milk or bread,
that horrible song of bodies without cloth or coverings,
the ominous song of the unsheltered
—sun and night dew—from the birth of day
until the death of life stretched out
in the impoverished section of a hospital.

Because, you should know,
that we know in fact this country starves.
Because we have heard and we have seen,
with these eyes that the earth shall swallow,
a mother asking for a half a pound of rice,
a half of beans, and a tail of dried codfish,
or half a pound of noodles
and two ounces of ham.

And that's not all.
We have seen the children drinking teas,
from the first scream until the father returns dirty from
 the sugarcane fields,
or the mother from a ball factory.
Or, on the contrary,
the father doing odd jobs during the off season
and the mother . . . the mother is . . . living.

The gentlemen poets shouldn't speak of sonnets, ten-line
 stanzas,
of transparencies, of literary contests, and of academies,
that these are merely excesses of youth.
The gentlemen's gentlemen, super poets, shouldn't say
that we aren't crying the song!

(Translated by Digna Sánchez-Méndez)

Ángela María Dávila (b. 1944)

acabo de morir . . .

acabo de morir,
y que mi muerte
sirva de grito hondo a mi garganta,
y que me arda la sal de tanto tiempo
prendida y afuegada.
acabo de morir,
y que mi muerte
se empuje ronca y fuerte por mis manos,
que la piel de mis venas se haga arterias,
que se encrespe naciéndome en mi sangre.
la muerte me llegó, así, de golpe
revolcándome pieles ya gastadas,
naciéndome en las ansias de anuevarme.
pobre en mí, por mis surcos
me levanta una aurora tambaleante;
por mis pasos perdidos,
por mi huella ingastable,
se me encauza la muerte a garrotazos
volcándome la vida.
¡vida yo!
con la aurora latiéndome en los pasos.

Para mi nombre quiero . . .

Para mi nombre quiero
sepultureros grises y tajantes.
Es más:
no quiero nombre,

i have just died . . .

i have just died,
let my death
serve as a deep cry to my throat,
and let the salt of so much time sting
lit and on fire.
i have just died
let my death
push hoarse and strong through my hands,
let the skin of my veins become arteries,
let it clench being born in my blood.
death arrived, just like that, suddenly
stirring up skins already spent
being born in the longing for renewal.
impoverished in me, a staggering dawn
lifts me by my furrows:
because of my lost steps,
because of my tracks unspent,
death takes over pounding
spilling my life.
life i!
with dawn pulsating in the steps.

(Translated by María Arrillaga)

I Want for My Name . . .

I want for my name
gray and cutting grave diggers.
Moreover:
I don't want a name,

que me lo lleve el mar lavándolo
en mi arena.
Que me lo arrastre el mar,
y que yo sienta
que estoy allí la intacta,
la sin nombre.
Que estoy allí, con vibración del golpe
de la ola.
Con mi sabor de sal,
con mi sabor de espuma,
temblante con sabor de verde mar.
A solas con mi piel y con mis valles,
con mis ojos adentro, con mis cuencas,
con mis playas ardientes,
recorrida en bandadas de murmullos,
desnombrada.
Sólo está el mar latente,
palpitándome amor de ola y arrullos . . .

let the sea take it washing it
in my sand.
Let the ocean drag it,
that I may feel
I am there intact,
without a name.
That I am there, with the vibrations of the blow
of the wave.
With my taste of salt
with my taste of foam,
shaking with the taste of the green sea.
Alone with my skin and with my valleys,
with my eyes inside, my river basins,
with my ardent shores,
gathered in flocks of murmurs
nameless.
The throbbing ocean is alone,
pulsating love of waves and lullabies . . .

(Translated by María Arrillaga)

Billy Cajigas (b. 1944)

Antinana

Mi hijo también tiene un nombre:
Se llama Guillermo.
Es gracioso.
Y no le teme a los poetas armados
que dan navajazos al tiempo,
a la vida, a la aurora y al viento.

Mi niño no llora
cuando ciento y pico de alfileres
se le clavan en el pecho.
¡Es cosquilloso mi niño Guillermo!

Si tiene los ojos azules
no es por parecer un ángel,
es porque nació con ellos.

Cuando moja los pañales (y los calienta),
y los ensucia . . . le huye a la rima
sin dejar de ser verso.

Entonces hay que velar a mi niño Guillermo
porque si no, se come la ñoña,
se embarra la boca, la nariz, los dedos . . .
¡Y hay que darle fuete a mi niño travieso!

Hágase el cobre

Para eso hay que llamarlos uno a uno.
Así.

Antilullaby

My son also has a name:
He's called Guillermo.
He's cute.
And he's not afraid of armed poets
that knife time,
life, sunrise, and the wind.

My son doesn't cry
When over a hundred pins
sink into his chest.
My son Guillermo is ticklish!

If he has blue eyes,
it's not because he looks like an angel,
it's because he was born with them.

When he wets his diapers (and warms them),
and defecates on them . . . he runs from the rhyme
without forgetting to be verse.

Then you have to watch my child Guillermo
because if not, he eats the crap
he daubs his mouth, his nose, his fingers. . . .
And you have to spank my mischievous child!

(Translated by Digna Sánchez-Méndez)

Let There Be Copper!

For that you have to call them one by one.
Like this.

O visitarlos.
Así.
Fácil . . . ¿verdad?

Y salió el primero de los hombres
con un enorme compás de espera
para sembrarlo en el mismo dolor de la historia.
(Peor si digo que fue en la tierra.)
Y consiguió más.
Tanto, que el tiempo se midió por la angustia,
y se cantó en la voz hueca de un ruiseñor
  portátil,
liviano.
Fácil . . . ¿verdad?

¿Y los otros?
Se quedaron allá, inquietos,
sonriendo y lamiendo estampillas aéreas.
Acelerando el proceso.

Uno a uno.
Así.
—La tierra no produce.
—¿No?
—Le pagamos el triple por su tierra.
El cobre es de baja calidad.
—¡¡Sí!!
(Y fue la primera vez que la tierra parió
  por los senos.)

Suerte que llegamos nosotros
hablando pestes de los yanquis.
—¡Oiga!, búsquese el fusil y combata al villano turista.

—Señor:
a mí no me preocupan los amigos
ni los extraños . . .
Solamente me preocupan los que me conocen de vista.

Or visit them.
Like this.
Easy . . . right?

And the first man came out
with an enormous compass of hope
to plant it in the very pain of history.
(Worse if I say it was in the earth.)
And he obtained more.
So much, that time was measured by anguish,
and it was sung in the empty voice of a portable
nightingale,
light.
Easy . . . right?

And the others?
They stayed there, restless,
smiling and licking air-mail stamps.
Accelerating the process.

One by one.
Like this.
"The earth doesn't produce."
"No?"
"We'll pay you triple for your land.
The copper is of low quality."
"Yes!"
(And it was the first time that the earth gave birth
through the breast.)

Lucky we came
speaking badly of the Yankees.
"Listen! get your gun and fight the villainous tourist."

"Sir:
I don't care about friends
or strangers. . . .
I only care about those that know me by sight."

(Translated by Digna Sánchez-Méndez)

Supongamos . . .

Si ahora mismo dijera: ¡CARAJO!
Así, por decirlo—por cualquier cosa—,
ustedes de seguro me perdonarían.
Y yo, claro, yo les pediría
en el nombre de la "pulcritud" que nos une,
en el nombre de los trajes,
de las corbatas,
de los relojes a prueba de agua,
de las iglesias preñadas por obra y gracia . . .
Yo les exigería
(y si me dejan lo cuelgo en un lugar visible):

¡FAVOR DE USAR EL ZAFACÓN
AL TIRAR SUS SONRISAS!

Entre nosotros

Ahora comienzas a entender mejor.
A ver:
Reconoces que la vida en la Colonia
es dura.
Que no es tan fácil después de casada.
Que te sacan el jugo en el trabajo,
en la fábrica,
y que muchas,
muchísimas obreras como tú sufren mareos . . .
Y sabes más (¡y si no,
debieras!).
Sabes que hay un día moviéndose,
colgando del pecho,
para las que han dejado su brillo
en un zapato,
para las que ya no pueden producir
más brasieres y guantes.

Let's Suppose . . .

If I said "Hell!" right now
Just to say it—for anything—
I'm sure you would forgive me.
And I, of course, would ask you
in the name of the "gentility" that unites us,
in the name of suits,
of ties,
of waterproof watches,
of churches begotten by the grace of . . .
I would demand
(and if you let me I'll hang it in a public place):

PLEASE USE THE TRASHCAN
WHEN THROWING AWAY SMILES!

(Translated by Digna Sánchez-Méndez)

Between Us

Now you're beginning to understand better.
Let's see:
You realize that life inside the Colony
is hard.
That it's not that easy after you're married.
That they bleed you at work,
in the factory,
and that many,
many workers suffer dizzy spells as you do . . .
And you know more than that (and if you don't,
you should).
You know that a day is moving,
hanging from the chest,
for those that left their shine
on a shoe,
for those that can no longer produce
more brassieres and gloves.

Una hora en hilachas,
para despedir a cualquiera
de las jornaleras.

Que otra intentará desde su miseria
hacer "lo mismo" que hizo Mary.
O como la que se sacó el muchacho
antes de que se corriera la voz
y la sorprendieran preñada de su esposo.
"Y para eso estaban los contraceptivos."

¿Entiendes ahora por qué
no podías jugar con tu cielo al azul?
¿Comprendes ahora por qué
debieras estar con mi dolor al rojo?

Sí . . . Ya sé que esto debería
quedarse "entre nosotros."
No hay problema, compañera.

El pobre Dios

Por fin viene Dios.
Está llegando a la Tierra,
sin ombligo. Nada huele a azufre
y no se ve la llama ardiente.
El Eterno Legislador por acumulación de las almas
está con nosotros.
Se mueve ahora entre la multitud.
La multitud lo aclama.
La multitud lo carga.
Saluda a lado y lado.
Angeles y arcángeles de pistolas
cargadas con agua bendita lo protegen.
Los muchachos de la prensa lo rodean.
Llueven las preguntas y Dios no las contesta.

One hour on loose threads,
to dismiss any
of the day laborers.

Who else would attempt in her misery
to do the same that Mary did.
Or like the one who aborted the child
before the word got around
and they found her pregnant by her husband.
"For that there were contraceptives."

Do you understand now why
you couldn't play the blue game with your sky?
Do you see now why
you should be with my pain at its sharpest?

Yes . . . I know this
should stay "between us."
No problem, *compañera.*

(Translated by Digna Sánchez-Méndez)

Poor God

God is finally coming.
He's arriving on earth,
without a belly button. Nothing smells of sulfur
nor do you see a burning flame.
The eternal legislator by accumulation of souls
is with us.
He's walking among the multitude.
The multitude acclaims him.
The multitude carries him.
He waves from side to side.
Angels and archangels with pistols
loaded with Holy Water protect him.
The boys of the press surround him.
Questions rain down but God doesn't answer them.

Un ángel con alas de papel de periódico
se acerca y dice:
—Dios ha perdido la razón.
Los periodistas quieren más detalles.
El ángel riposta:
—Señores, éste no es el fin del mundo.
Es un simulacro.

* *

La nariz del M-1 resopla una balahostia:
—Le volaron la tapa de los sesos a Dios.
(The New York Times.)
Una ambulancia celestial lo lleva en volandas:
Guiándola va su ángel de la guarda.
(El Mundo, edición vespertina.)

* * *

Un millón de ángelesmédicoscirujanos
cosen alrededor de su cuello.
Al fin logran pegar su cabeza.

* * * *

Insistía en volver a la Tierra.
Quería hablar del Amor,
de la igualdad entre los hombres,
de la paz . . . de los sepulcros.

* * * * *

Llegó a decirlo,
pero nadie le creyó.
Todos cruzaron por un puente de embuste.
El Pobre se sonrojó.
El pobre San Dios
sentía que la cara
se le estaba cayendo nuevamente,
esta vez de la vergüenza.

An angel with newspaper wings
approaches and says:
"God has lost his reason."
The newspapermen want more details.
The angel answers back:
"Gentlemen, this is not the end of the world.
It's a drill."

* *

The nose of the M-1 snorts a eucharistic bullet:
"They blew God's brains out."
(*The New York Times.*)
A celestial ambulance carries him through the air:
His guardian angel is driving it.
(*El Mundo*, evening edition.)

* * *

A million medicsurgeonangels
sew around his neck.
They're finally able to join his head.

* * * *

He insisted on returning to earth.
He wanted to talk of love,
of equality among men,
of peace . . . of sepulchers.

* * * * *

He got to say it,
but no one believed him.
All crossed over a bridge of lies.
The poor thing blushed.
Poor Saint God
he felt his head
hanging again,
this time in shame.

(Translated by Digna Sánchez-Méndez)

Iván Silén (b. 1944)

Es la una y cuarto . . .

Es la una y cuarto
de un nueve de julio en la ciudad de Nueva York,
y es tan fácil comprender la vocación,
es como sentarse en la ventana
y mirar hacia afuera
y oir que Van Gogh dice que se va a
suicidar,
y comprenderlo así,
como si dijera merci,
y oir un piano en clave de sol
como si lo tocara Dios,
y saber que muy pronto
los médicos me prohibirán escribir,
hasta que me cure,
pero eso es como subirle el volumen
al radio y oir la música más fuerte,
y saber que soy un
valley of the dolls
la muerte—la locura
l'aimer the sex,
y saber que mi casa es un Blow-up
y que yo tengo la cara pintada de blanco,
como si fuera una gaviota
sobre un vaso de leche
o sobre la sábana,
y descubrir de momento
que uno tiene las manos sucias,
y recordar que Chiclana fuma
marihuana todos los días y ya no pinta,
y encerrarme en mi cuarto
y resucitar al Ché
o la Maga,
y querer gritar una mala palabra,
y saber que estoy acusado de conspiración,
y ver en la nevera un no exit,

It's One-fifteen . . .

It's one-fifteen
on a 9th of July in the city of New York
and it's so easy to understand one's vocation,
it's like sitting by the window
and looking out
and hearing that Van Gogh says he's going to commit
suicide,
and understand it like this
as if he said *merci,*
and listening to a piano in G
as if God were playing it
and to know that very soon
the doctors will keep me from writing,
until I'm cured,
but that's like raising the volume of
the radio and listening to the music even louder
and knowing that I am a
valley of the dolls
death–insanity
l'aimer the sex
and knowing that my house is a Blow-up
and I have my face painted white
as if I were a gull
over a glass of milk
or on the sheet
and discovering suddenly
that one has dirty hands,
and remembering that Chiclana smokes
pot every day and no longer paints,
and closing myself in my room
and resuscitating Ché
or La Maga
and wanting to scream out a dirty word
and knowing that I am charged with conspiracy
and seeing in the icebox *no exit,*

y en el suelo un diccionario,
y no entender la órbita de la tierra,
ni por qué las cosas son como son
ni por qué yo escribo todos los días,
y recordar el cristo en el Parque Central
con una calavera sobre los hombros
y una campana entre las piernas,
y saber que la maquinilla está dañada
y las cosas no salen
como en el sexo cuando a uno le duele la espalda,
y pensar que voy en una guagua,
aunque tengo que lavar la ropa,
y voy viajando,
y releo el Corno Emplumado y Agudelo me saluda,
y me dan deseos de tomar café
y le digo al siquiatra que voy a regresar
a mi apartamento,
y cierro la puerta
y él escribe en su récord:
¡SICOPATA!

Cristo—1970

Me he sentado dentro de la burocracia
para saber que todas las moscas se han quitado las alas
y sentir que la soledad y las arañas hablan
francés en la esquinas
y saber que afuera llueve o se caen las hojas
y ver aunque no vea
una muñeca en otro sitio que se quita ya losojos
y se sonríe por los dedos
por la mescalina que se escapa
por las puertas de una cara que reflejan los espejos
y yo me sonrío desde mi ombligo
o desde un subway que rompe la ilusión
desde la punta de mi lápiz
y él se asusta en otro cielo largo de metales
y otras lunas de otros lobos
por paredes ya sembradas en el cráneo de los niños
por los ríos que se inflan como globos en los parques

and a dictionary on the floor
and not understanding the earth's orbit,
nor why things are as they are
nor why I write every day,
and remembering the christ in Central Park
with a skull over his shoulder
and a bell between his legs,
and knowing that the typewriter is broken
and nothing works out
like in sex when one's back aches,
and thinking that I'm in a bus
though I have to wash my clothes,
and I travel,
and I reread *el Corno Emplumado* and Agudelo greets me
and I feel like drinking coffee
and I tell the psychiatrist that I'm going back
to my apartment,
and I close the door
and he writes on his record:
PSYCHOPATH!

(Translated by Ellen G. Matilla)

Christ—1970

I have sat myself inside bureaucracy
to know that all the flies have shed their wings
and to feel that solitude and spiders speak
french on the corners
and to know that outside it rains or the leaves are falling
and to see although not look
a doll in another place that has already put out her eyes
and laughs through her fingers
the mescaline that flees
through the doors of a face in reflected mirrors
and I smile from my navel
or from a subway that breaks the illusion
from my pencil point
and he is frightened in another long sky of metals
and other moons of other wolves
by walls already planted in the minds of children
in rivers that swell like balloons in parks

y tal vez otras ciudades
levantadas por las cruces
o en otros cigarrillos
un amor sobre los rifles
que nos muerda en las axilas
y esa cara que se rompe de tiempo en los cristales
y en losojos de las ratas
nos sorprende por la lengua y en pasillos clausurados
o en un adiós de algún profeta en la lascivia de una monja
o en un santo por su culo
en su canción de maravilla
o todos los poetas por mi mano izquierda hacia la nada
y esa cara todavía en el dial del teléfono
o en el sonido grabado de una palabra-rota
que se sigue haciendo rara por los muebles y las cosas
y por la cara Cristo al abordaje
cantando por losojos o en cada cerradura
la muerte que no llega
y todo se detiene en los pasos de un extraño
y sus manos de abanico por los cuerpos de los niños
y los ángeles de cartón por sus rosas de cristales
anunciándome en la locura que debo retornar
y entonces vuelvo por mis muertos
grito-a-grito
por la niebla dura de las alas derretidas
y arrastro poblado en mariposas los oídos
y vengo poco-a-poco cargado de figuras
y golpe a golpe en golondrinas
y sangre a sangre, así,
por las nalgas
por los senos
por las manos de una virgen toda herida. . . .

El pájaro-loco

A Pedro Pietri

Bajamos hacia donde siempre es peligroso que se baje
hacia donde hay tantas alcantarillas cerradas todavía
tantos recovecos

and maybe other cities
raised by crosses
or in other cigarettes
a love over rifles
that chews us in the armpits
and that face which breaks with time in crystals
and in the eyes of the rats
surprises us in the tongue of closed corridors
or in a farewell of some prophet to a nun's lust
or in a saint through the ass
in his miracle song
or all the poets by my left hand toward nothing
and that face still in the telephone dial
or in the recorded sound of a broken word
that keeps being strange by the furniture and things
and by the face of Christ on the attack
singing through the eyes or in each lock
death that does not come
and all stops at the steps of a stranger
and his fanlike hands over the bodies of children
and the cardboard angels with their crystal roses
telling me in madness that I must return
and then I come back for my dead
howling
through the hard fog with melted wings
and I drag my ears full of butterflies
and I come little by little loaded with figures
and blow by blow in swallows
and blood to blood, like this,
by the buttocks
by the breasts
by the hands of a wounded virgin. . . .

(Translated by Ellen G. Matilla)

Woody Woodpecker

To Pedro Pietri

We descend where there is always danger going down
toward where there are still so many closed drains
so many labryinths

despacio
mientras yo tejo mi retorno
con los hilos del silencio
ahora que bajamos escaleras apagadas
donde hay ángeles horribles con cara de
pasado
donde hay cajas cerradas de murmullos
despacio
que las puertas están cerradas por los caminos
del miedo
y hay mil pájaros ciegos cantando
la mañana
a la entrada de las puertas esperando
para abrir de momento losojos de la muerte
y se rompan los cristales de misojos
mientras los monjes de la noche
hacen de los vidrios molidos una verdad que yo recito
en estos túneles
de espejos y de caras
que dan a una mañana larga de humo
a una mañana donde hay hombres atravesados por
relámpagos eternos
y sus cuerpos se consumen por el fuego
mientras se derrite la noche
sobre sus bocas de cera
¡todo es monstruoso!
pero hemos llegado a la ciudad maldita
y toda la ciudad es un canto de ceniza
todo Nueva York es un grito sin sonido
y los túneles se abren hacia arriba
como si fueran árboles de otoño
pero yo sigo mis propios callejones
donde los seres se emborrachan
con los sexos opuestos
y corre el semen como si fuera vino
como si fuera la crema de un niño que se derrama
así entro a las tabernas y a los bares de mis sueños
donde se hace la revolución como si se hicieran los zapatos
donde está el político que se masturba al aire-libre
y las monjas recogen los genes para el próximo santo
así vuelan los sesos sobre las manos de un niño

slowly
while I weave my return
with threads of silence
now that we descend dark stairs
where there are horrible angels with a face of
the past
where there are closed boxes of sighs
slowly
'cause the doors are closed by the paths
of fear
and there are one thousand blind birds singing
the morning
waiting at the entrance of the doors
to open suddenly the eyes of death
and the crystals of my eyes break
while the monks of the night
make from the ground glass a truth I recite
in these tunnels
of mirrors and of faces
that face a long morning of smoke
to a morning where there are men pierced by
eternal lightning
and their bodies are consumed by fire
while the night melts
over their waxen mouths
everything is monstrous
but we have reached the damned city
and the whole city is a song of ashes
all New York is a soundless scream
and the tunnels open face up
as if they were autumn trees
but I follow my own alleys
where people get drunk
with the opposite sex
and the semen runs like wine
like the spilling cream of a child
like that I enter the taverns and the bars of my dreams
where revolution is made like shoes
where the politician masturbates in the open air
and the nuns collect genes for the next saint
like that the brains fly over the hands of a child

y todos cantan al suicida que amanece
y Nueva York todavía es más largo
pero yo sigo mi camino como caperucita
diciendo mi cuento viejo
hasta la puerta del ahorcado
hasta la puerta de la lesbiana que vende frutas tropicales
en esta capital del mundo
que yo veo desde este túnel
desde la ventana de misojos
y oigo mis latidos como si fueran tambores
y releo a Rilke y le digo hermano
oyendo un coro que dice "sigue-sigue"
porque Nueva York tiene
siete ángeles castrados
con siete copas divinas para el juicio de la viuda
que viene en su cádilac tirado por caballos
y en cada caballo un ángel
y en cada ángel una espada
y en cada espada una virgen atravesada por los senos
pero a mí nada me importa
yo—soy el insensible
el que me rio callado
el que camino con botas
pisando los silencios que de los árboles se han caído
y las cabezas cortadas que caen en la canasta
donde duerme mi niño
así camino hasta las tumbas abiertas
y mi madre me invita a un desayuno
mientras Prometeo le mete la mano entre las piernas
y todas las madres se persignan
¡ay la envidia!
pero Nueva York es más bello todavía
hay hoteles donde te cortan las manos
y te entierran clavos sagrados por losojos
para que los militares no se cansen de cansancio
mientras leen a Hemingway
con manos mohosas de alfileres
y guardan una libreta enorme
de hojas que se rompen
por la lista de maricones azulitos
porque todavía hay penicilina

and everyone sings to the dawning suicide
and New York is still longer
but I follow my road like little red riding hood
repeating my old story
up to the door of the hanged
up to the door of the lesbian who sells tropical fruits
in this capital of the world
that I see from this tunnel
from the window of my eyes
and I hear my heart beat like drums
and I reread Rilke and I call him a brother
hearing a chorus saying "go on—go on"
because New York has
seven castrated angels
with seven divine cups for the trial of the widow
who comes in her cadillac pulled by horses
and on each horse an angel
and on each angel a sword
and on each sword a virgin speared through her breasts
but I couldn't care less
me—I am insensitive
the one who laughs silently
the one who walks with boots
stepping on the silence fallen from the trees
and the decapitated heads which fall in the basket
where my child sleeps
like that I walk to the open graves
and my mother invites me to breakfast
while Prometheus feels her up
and all mothers cross themselves
oh, the envy!
but New York is still more beautiful
there are hotels where they cut your hands
and they bury secret nails in your eyes
so that the military do not tire of tiredness
while they read Hemingway
with pin-rusted hands
and keep a huge notebook
with pages that tear
at the list of little blue faggots
because there is still penicillin

mientras la orina no sale
como si se hubieran pillado un dedo
al bajarse del último taxi
y la sangre coagulada
y los coros se amontonan sobre Broadway
"en la cruz en la cruz
do primero vi la luz"
son los judíos o los cristianos
que no conocen la luz eléctrica
pero seguimos bajando
porque hay un pájaro-loco
que toca la guitarra
que sabotea
que mata
que mete
entonces oigo una gran voz
como la que se oye en el poema de Ernesto
Cardenal
oigo una gran voz
que me dice
que te dice
este poema está prohibido
en puerto rico
y lo anuncia la radio
la prensa
el cura desde el templo
lo dice en la escuela
se prohibe . . . titititi . . . se prohibe . . .
todo esto en teletipo
pero me doy cuenta de mi embuste y sigo andando
mientras las niñas tiemblan de placer
cantan un aleluya por mi cara
mientras sus vulvas se humedecen por la lluvia
y oigo sus voces más claras
como si hablaran por los altoparlantes
oigo sus voces que dicen:
"dónde va el loquito
que-minuflí que minuflá"
pero yo no hago caso
pues yo no soy ningún don juan
porque sólo busco una monja para que haya más lascivia

while the urine doesn't flow
as if they squashed a finger
getting off the last taxi
and the blood coagulated
and the choruses pile up on Broadway
"on the cross on the cross
where I first saw the light"
they are the jews or the christians
who don't know the electric light
but keep descending
because there is a woody woodpecker
that plays the guitar
that sabotages
that kills
that fucks
then I hear a big voice
like the one in the poem of Ernesto
Cardenal
I hear a big voice
that says
that says
this poem is forbidden
in Puerto Rico
and the radio announces it
the press
the priest from the church
they say it in school
it's forbidden . . .tititi . . . it's forbidden
all this in teletype
but I realize my lie and keep going
while girls shake with pleasure
they sing a hallelujah for my face
while their vulvas are moistened by the rain
and I hear their voices more clearly
as if through a loudspeaker
I hear their voices that say:
"donde va el loquito
que-minuflí-que-minuflá"
but I don't pay attention
I am no Don Juan
I'm only looking for a nun so I can be more lecherous

y así soñando doblo hacia la sexta avenida
buscando la paz de los sepulcros
pero hay una multitud que avanza en carretera
que avanza en ratonera de cantazo
gritando
jíbaro-sí yanqui-no
mientras se tocan las nalgas unos a otros
y yo lo tengo que decir aunque todo el mundo lo sabe
entonces el milagro me llega por losojos
y descubro a Orfeo con su coito con Eurídices
pero Orfeo está loco
y grita que todas las mujeres son su ninf
violando las noches de otoño
ultrajando la brisa y los caminos
y Orfeo está loco
Orfeo es un enfermo—grita la gente
y yo lo paro en el camino
lo abrazo como si fuera mi padre
pero él me empuja violento
y me grita y ustedes lo oyen
y me grita: ¡deja poeta!
así se pierde gritando el estribillo
pero a mí no me importa nada
porque yo-soy el que soy
el que tengo la llave de mi verso
y un revólver 38 en el bolsillo
así camino este Nueva York moderno
hasta encontrarme a los burócratas vomitando
sillas y papeles por la boca
como si fuera una escena de Fellini
mientras alguien grita "corten"
entonces entran los burgueses hemofílicos
desangrándose de tantas horas iguales como siempre
y la misma voz que grita "corten"
y descubro de momento que es por mí
que la gente se amotina
y me exigen que me calle
mientras yo sigo bailando
mi baile que no acaba
cantando mi angustia
que termina en los caminos

and dreaming thus I turn toward sixth avenue
looking for the peace of the grave
but there is a crowd advancing on the road
advancing in a mousetrap
yelling
jíbaro-yes yankee-no
while they touch each other's asses
and I have to say it although everyone knows it
then the miracle reaches me through my eyes
and I discover Orpheus in coitus with Eurydice
but Orpheus is crazy
and screams that all women are his
violating nights of autumn
raping the breeze and the roads
and Orpheus is crazy
"Orpheus is sick," screams the people
and I stop him on the road
I embrace him as if he were my father
but violent he pushes me away
and yells at me and you all hear it
he yells at me: "forget it poet"
and he disappeared yelling the refrain
but I couldn't care less
because I—I am who I am
he who has the key to my verse
and a 38 in my pocket
like that I walk this modern New York
until I meet the bureaucrats vomiting
chairs and papers through their mouths
as if it were a scene from Fellini
while someone calls "cut"
then enter the hemophiliac bourgeoisie
bleeding from so many hours the same as always
and the same voice that calls "cut"
and I suddenly discover that it is because of me
that people are rioting
and demanding my silence
while I keep dancing
my dance that never ends
singing my anguish
that finished on the roads

en todos mis dedos que se llenan de noche
como si se llenaran de pus
para siempre
entonces me quito mi antifaz
hasta mi rostro de tristeza
y rio mi tristeza larga
como una avenida niuyorquina
hasta detenerme en la puerta de mi casa
en la alcantarilla que está frente a mi casa
y ver y no ver nada
como un recuerdo largo
como si todo fuera un sueño
un sueño de amor bastante largo . .

La luna ofendida

Yo también tengo una levita
como la que usara Pushkin
y un Padre Nuestro mejor que el de Neruda
y me llevo a Nueva York en el bolsillo
como lo dejara Lorca
alborotando las calles de silencio
las camino paso-a-paso
con mis maletas de papeles preparadas al olvido
así te dejo Nueva York
ataúd de tantosojos colectivos
me voy por un cojón de deseos
porque soy azul como una nube
y creo en la poesía como se cree en los cheques
cacerola vieja de mis sueños
ciudad de café instantáneo
yo tengo una bolsita llena de cristales
y un poema nuevo en cada ojo
en cada ojo de botella
que yo me saco desfigurando mi rostro de vidriales
como estalactitas quebradas me quito losojos
y recibo una carta de un librero de lejos
que me da la noticia
haciendo callejones

on all my fingers that fill with night
as if they were filled with pus
forever
then I leave my mask
up to my face of sadness
and I laugh my long sadness
like a New York avenue
until I stop at the door of my house
at the sewer in front of my house
and to see and not see anything
like a long memory
as if all were a dream
a long long dream of love . . .

(Translated by Ellen G. Mati[illegible])

The Offended Moon

I also have tails
like those worn by Pushkin
and a better Our Father than that of Neruda
and I carry New York in my pocket
as Lorca left it
making noise in the streets of silence
I walk them step by step
with my luggage filled with papers packed for oblivion
thus I leave you New York
coffin of so many collective eyes
I'm leaving because my balls feel like it
because I am blue like a cloud
and I believe in poetry like some believe in checks
stale casserole of my dreams
city of instant coffee
I have a little bagful of crystals
and a new poem in each eye
in each bottle eye
that I remove disfiguring my stain glass face
like broken stalactites I take off my eyes
and I receive a letter from a bookseller far away
who writes
making alley ways

por mis venas
enmohecidas de nada
que me da la noticia
y me dice
que mis versos le han
gustado a una niña
que no se acuesta conmigo
porque no soy un Lord Byron
porque tengo una copa de sangre que darle
y todos los días asesino palomas
yo la mordería entre las piernas
como si fuera una manzana de una tarde cualquiera
la mordería como he mordido el crepúsculo
por esa calle del alba
y dejaría los espejos de tristeza
mientras camino los posters cansado
sintiendo que me pican los sobacos
como si trajera pájaros dormidos en los ganglios
por este sudor que corre en desodorantes prestados
ENTONCES LE DIRÍA QUE EL SUICIDIO ES UNA MANO QUE
ESCRIBE TODO EL DÍA
le diría
lkjhgfdsa/$"=&!?
mientras cazo la luna
como quien caza mariposas—roídas
y la alimento con vidrio y fósforo molido
y la cazo desnuda de miedo
por su cuerpo en el río reflejando su vulva
de ramas caídas
de estrellas podridas de luces
como quien craquea estrellas borradas
como quien trazara la noche en papeles de copia
así he violado
rompiendo los dedos de vitrinas ausentes
rompiendo distancia de niña-marchita
de niña-azul-por-su-culo-botella
de cenicienta mi verso que gusta susojos
y me lo dijo el librero
y por eso lo digo
niña que me puedes robar este verso
mi corazón es de alambre que da a la guerra

through my veins
rusted from nothing
who writes
and tells me
that a girl has
liked my poems
that she won't sleep with me
because I'm not Lord Byron
because I have a cup of blood to give her
and every day I murder pigeons
I would bite her between the legs
as if she were an apple of any afternoon
I would bite her like I have bitten dusk
on that street of dawn
and I would leave the mirrors of sadness
while tired I walk the posters
feeling that my armpits itch
as if I were carrying sleeping birds in my ganglions
through this sweat that runs in borrowed deodorants
THEN I WOULD TELL HER THAT SUICIDE IS A HAND THAT
WRITES ALL DAY
I would tell her
lkjhgfdsa/$" &!?
while I hunt the moon
like one who chases gnawed butterflies
and I feed her with crushed glass and phosphorus
and I chase her naked with fear
her body in the river reflecting her vulva
of falling branches
of rotten stars of lights
as one that cracks erased stars
as one who traces night in carbon paper
like so I have raped
breaking the fingers of the absent store windows
breaking the distance of withering girl
of girl-blue-through-her-ass
of cinderella my poem that her eyes like
and the bookseller told me
and so I say
girl you who can steal this poem from me
my heart is of wire that faces war

y mi aorta se abre como un abrelatas
que bombea mi sangre maldita de rata
y te lo digo niña como quien habla a una nube
te pareces a mí con tu soberbia de loca
te lo digo
aunque mi poema me costara la cárcel
te lo digo
que en la cama soy un sueño que no acaba
mientras te lleno tusojos de alfileres
y te corren aguas de cuneta y
cuneta
por tanto mimo amontonado
por tus días de basura y de blanquita
te lo digo con corazón de comunista
en tus narices de muñeca de palacio
te lo canto como un Romeo
de callejones que no has visto
te lo canto a ti
a quien le han gustado mis versos
a ti niña ciega
que no ves que entre tu cuerpo y mi cuerpo
hay una revolución que se acaba
y un crimen que me espera aplaudiendo caminos
ciega de tantos libros y salones
no ves que has pecado mi cabeza que computa y que computa
que me río otra rima
que me burlo otra muerte
en esta carcajada tan larga
en que traigo mi verso a mi correr de sangre
y me río como un Dimitri moderno que no teme tu
ira
y si se moviera tu mano contra mi cabeza de trapo
la cárcel sería un escándalo bello donde amanecen cristales
donde dolería tu lengua
donde mi libro seguiría arrastrando
sus zapatos roídos y sus puntos y sus siglos
y mil comas de penes levantadas al cielo
como se levanta a dios este signo de guerra.

and my artery opens like a can opener
that pumps my damn rat blood
and I tell you girl as I would speak to a cloud
you look like me with your arrogance of madness
I tell you
although my poem will cost me imprisonment
I tell you
that in bed I am a dream that doesn't end
while I fill your eyes with pins
and you overflow with waters running from sewer to sewer
with so many caresses
for your days of garbage and of pretense
I tell you with the heart of a communist
in your doll's nose of palaces
I sing it like a Romeo
of alleys you haven't seen
I sing it to you
to the one who has liked my poems
to you blind girl
who doesn't see that between your body and my body
there is a revolution which is ending
and a crime that awaits me applauding roads
blind one of so many books and parlors
don't you see that you have sinned my head that clicks and clicks
that I laugh another rhyme
that I mock another death
in this long long laugh
in which I bring my poem to my flow of blood
and I laugh like a modern Dimitri who doesn't fear your wrath
and if your hand were to move against my head of rag
prison would be a beautiful scandal where crystals dawn
where your tongue would ache
where my book would still be crawling
its beat-up shoes and its periods and its centuries
and one thousand comas of penes raised to the sky
like the sign of war is raised to God.

(Translated by Ellen G. Matilla)

Edwin Reyes Berríos (b. 1944)

Inés el viento . . .

INÉS el viento
el mar a veces
cuando uno silba solo
calle abajo y el lujo presuroso
de recordar los pájaros serenos de mi barrio
impasible a esta hora de plomo tú mirabas
hoja ardiente crecía el silencio
y el humo Inés la tarde el arco deslumbrante
    de la playa y su diálogo remoto
                de peces como labios
        sucesivos
ritos del corazón y la memoria
        desatada perpetua
más allá de este extraño mediodía
dos amigos te nombran pensativos
                                    te buscan
en el café con frío de las tres
    y la muerte
fija en su noche única tus pasos
la torre el sol la torre abandonada
borrada a ras del alba como las tentaciones
y Buenos Aires pasa Inés la bruma
el milagro amarillo de las desiertas alas sobre el mar
                                                repetida
tu imagen en su espejo infatigable
de niña arrodillada estremecida siembras
las astromelias brujas de esa tarde
en que escuchaba a Bach como desde tu frente
dejaba que mi cuerpo que la flama que el honrado total
                                        oficio de la fiera
                        recorríamos
la casi diminuta infinitud del aire

Inés the Wind . . .

INÉS the wind
the sea sometimes
when one whistles alone
down the street and the hasty luxury
of remembering the unruffled birds of my neighborhood
unmoved at this leaden hour you were looking at
burning leaf the silence was growing
and the smoke Inés the afternoon the blazing arch
  of the beach and its remote dialogue
                          of fish like lips
    successive
rites of heart and memory
    forever unbound
beyond this strange noon
two friends name you thoughtful
                                    they search for you
in the cold coffee at three o'clock
  and death
fixes your steps on her only night
the tower the sun the abandoned tower
erased even with the dawnlike temptations
and Buenos Aires passes Inés the mist
the yellow miracle of the barren wings over the sea
                                          repeated
your image in its untiring mirror
of trembling girl kneeling you seed
the bewitching astromelias of that afternoon
when I was listening to Bach as if from your forehead
I let my body the flame of the whole honest
                              craft of the beast
                  we traveled over
the almost minute infinity of air

para volver Inés como los marineros
de ceniza los ojos tendrás
y el mundo   martes
como este cigarrillo que se apaga y se apaga

Se dice que la mano oscura mía . . .

SE DICE QUE la mano oscura mía
mata y siembra sus cosas
precipitado el hombre asume formas busca
el banquillo exhala el humo tarde
bajaré hasta la plaza me miraré
en el árbol como mi abuelo el alto que guardaba
palomas en sus ojos arrozales remotos recorría
el murmullo dorado de la luz
en las trémulas hojas
el manatial redondo entre fusiles
                suspendido en la tarde
        busqué como los ángeles
el signo aterrador de mi cabeza
dominio de ancha selva
aliado de la lluvia amé caminos largos
corrientes poderosas hallé la risotada
los ojos babeantes del más reciente fusilado
sabiendo que mis cosas la boca abierta el polvo
nada tienen que ver con el hedor helado
de estos cuerpos que palpo los diminutos
puentes que la muerte coloca estos rostros
de yeso para brindar mi vaso
como el ávido yanqui alcemos
                como el bárbaro
nuestra propia y desierta calavera

to return Inés like the ashen
sailors the eyes you will have
and the world   Tuesday
like this cigarette that dies out and dies out

(Translated by Ellen G. Matilla)

They Say That My Dark Hand . . .

THEY SAY THAT my dark hand
kills and sows its things
man rushed takes forms looks for
the little bench exhales smoke late
I will go down to the plaza I will look at myself
in the tree like my grandfather the tall one who kept
pigeons in his eyes the golden murmur of light
travelled over distant paddies
in the quivering leaves
the round spring among rifles
          suspended in the afternoon
     I searched like angels
the terrifying sign of my head
domain of wide jungle
ally of the rain I loved long roads
powerful currents I found the roar of laughter
the driveling eyes of the man most recently executed
knowing that my things mouth open dust
have nothing to do with the frozen stench
of these bodies that I touch the tiny
bridges that death arranges these plaster
faces to offer my glass
as the greedy yankee lets toast
          as the barbarian
our own and deserted skull

(Translated by Ellen G. Matilla)

ebrio de mí hacia mí . . .

ebrio de mí hacia mí lo que me sobra
aspiro hasta borrarme la cabeza
          volver
sobre la rueda atroz del instante
subido al alto al mísero consuelo
de conocerme grito entre las bestias
          hecho papel y signos
          hecho papel y signos
trazo
fantasmas cascos
del centurión sangriento enardece
tu tropa Marco el corazón
de tus caballos la distancia
febril del arco al vientre [illegible]
                    mañana entre cuchillos
como los hijos de tus redentores
                         hablo
para la plaza de los muertos
no el nombre que enterramos
no la estatua sino su forma
          los remos de tu barca
                    enciende
hoguera tras hoguera tras hoguera
hasta que sólo quede de ti la mansedumbre
                    el humo tenaz
          entre los parias
sufre camino sufre hasta la transparencia
muerde tus manos príncipe
          exquisito y nostálgico
mueca de ti hacia ti
los reyes ebrios marchan

high on me toward me . . .

high on me toward me what I have left over
I inhale until I cloud my head
to go back
over the terrible wheel of the moment
raised to the height to the miserable comfort
of knowing myself I yell among the beasts
made paper and signs
made paper and signs
I outline
ghosts' helmets
of the bleeding centurion incite
your troops Marco the heart
of your horses the fever h
distance of the arch to the stomach you will learn
tomorrow among knives
like sons of your redeemers
I speak
for the forum of the dead
not the name that we buried
not the statue but its form
the oars of your boats
light up
blaze after blaze after blaze
until only the tameness of you is left
the stubborn smoke
among the outcasts
suffer through endless roads suffer up to transparency
bite your hands exquisite
and nostalgic prince
grimace of you toward you
the drunken kings march away

(Translated by Ellen G. Matilla)

Ángel Luis Méndez (b. 1944)

pronombres del pasaje

deidad azul es la sonrisa
metal luz viento
pedazos de horas escondidos en los dientes de los muertos
nadie llama a las puertas del almuerzo
ni a las latas de sopa que reparten las ganancias del
sistema
one, two, three
—alguien cayó del edificio—
—lo tiraron porque no pagó—
se perdió detrás de la noche del ruego
nunca escuchado
ellos todos fuera de la tierra
verde ancha grande pura limpia suave
todos ellos AFUERA!!!!!
pedro se tuvo que ir, lo debía todo
y después quiso comprar un carro
se quedó en el atolladero
las principales ruedas del avión
las cajas rotas en el vuelo
desde aquí se sentía la diferencia
manolo dejó de ser manolo—se convirtió en 0
las mesas los calderos los nombres propios los sujetos
brincó la cerca tarde—tiene un tiro en la nuca
pillado en las ruedas de abridor de los trenes
ella siempre espera el cheque en la puerta de entrada
el aquél ellos todos nosotros tú
el 1*ro.* y el 16
001 016—combínalo
detrás se llenó su cuerpo de semillas
del zafacón y la basura
nadie pudo decir palabra— another one doctor?
y la música tremenda sílaba de sueño

pronouns of passage

deity blue is the smile
metal light wind
fragments of hours hidden in the teeth of the dead
no one rings at the doors of lunch
nor at the soup cans distributed with the profits of the
  system
one, two, three
"someone fell from the roof"
"they pushed him because he didn't pay"
he was lost behind the night of entreaty
never listened
all of them outside of earth
green wide big pure clean gentle
all of them OUT!!!!!
pedro had to leave, he owed everything
and later he wanted to buy a car
he stayed in the hole
the main wheels of the plane
the broken boxes on the flight
from here one could feel the difference
manolo stopped being manolo—he became 0
the tables the pots the proper names the subjects
he jumped the fence too late—he's been shot in the neck
pinned by the church-key wheels of the trains
she is always waiting for the check at the main entrance
he that one they all of us you
the first and the 16th
001 016—combine them
behind his body was filled with seeds
from the ash-can and the garbage
no one could say a word—*another one doctor?*
and the music tremendous syllable of dream

él se mueve, él se mueve toda su vida
palidez de huevo frío
comprar la vuelta a la esquina—la ida de nuevo al vientre
5 10 15 20
30 40 50
cerrando a cada paso las venas azules
dejando la verdad y hasta los cementerios
y recordar: lo grande es ir con pan am.

áurea petra maría

la tarde en este vecindario de casa sin destruirse
las intersecciones, las luces del parque prendidas por el sol
el cine que todavía cuesta un peso en la tanda de las doce
si me levanto temprano—el poema que se arrastra en la frente
y los bolsillos, la mancha en la punta de los dedos
el atrecho poco transitado—el darse el lujo de ser hombre
el hablar con maría, con áurea, con petra, tomarles un café
dos tres—aceptarles un pedazo de pan con mantequilla
oirlas decir muchas cosas—del ahorro, de las ganas de siempre
eso se traduce en un viaje en avión, una casita y un chequecito seguro
preguntar, dale recuerdos—que cómo está, como los pobres son
las palomas descalzas en los parques, los perros que no entienden
los regaños de sus amos que platican a unos ladridos tostados
por el frío y las latas de carne de caballo
el doblar la expresión en cualquier esquina—este paisaje de hombres

he moves, he moves all his life
pallor of a cold egg
to buy going around the corner—the return to the womb
5 10 15 20
30 40 50
closing at each step the blue veins
leaving the truth and even the cemeteries
and remembering: pan am makes the going great.

(Translated by Ellen G. Matilla)

áurea petra maría

the afternoon in this neighborhood of undestroyed houses
the intersections, the lights of the park lit by the
sun
the movie that is still a buck at twelve o'clock noon
if I get up early—the poem that crawls on the
forehead
and the pockets, the stain on the fingertips
the little-traveled shortcut, the luxury of being a man
to speak with maría, with áurea, with petra, to have a
coffee off of them
two three—accept from them a piece of bread and butter
to hear them say many things—of their savings, of what
they always want to do
that translates to a plane trip, a little house and a steady
little check
to ask, to give him my regards, I mean how is he, as the
poor are
the pigeons barefoot in the parks, the dogs that don't understand
the reprimands of their masters who chat with some barks
toasted
by the cold and the cans of horse meat
to crease the expression on any corner—this landscape of
men

cuatro faroles de cemento, cuatro cordeles que empujan
a la muerte
regresar a un caliente más escondido—sentarse y escribir
en esta maquinilla
hasta que proteste la radio, la lámpara o la televisión
que se encenderá a las seis para oir lo que ha sucedido en
el mundo
qué habrá sucedido? porque en este barrio ha sucedido
todo.

iniciales

poner un letrero en esta puerta cerrada
es llenarla de cintas y dibujos quebrados
que nunca nadie entenderá.

pretender silenciar los ojos de la muerte
las calamidades que azotan y procuran los ojos, los labios
detrás de las escaleras, delante de los autobuses
con unas manos de frío, flacas ante la noticia de lo nuevo
encontrarse aislado ante la variedad, varado a las
sonrisas
—el sol es una chapa roja en el cielo que se quedó pálida
y de pronto la apagaron—
izar la bandera del sudor ante la gracia de los niños
como quien levanta el sueño de cualquier cama
encontrar el lugar blando de los asientos de la tarde
que trae los cobradores, el ruido, el baño caliente,
los platos de arroz y la misma esquina rosa . . .
tratar de poner la mano sobre todos los sueños quedos y
sin nombre
regresar por las noches al vacío que producen las tardes
de sol
cuando penetran a los rincones donde se quedó en cu-
clillas
una espera, un recado, una llamada, un vaso de ron, una
nota en la puerta

four cement street lights, four strings pushing toward death
to return to a warmth more hidden—to sit down and write on this typewriter
until the radio protests, the lamp or the television
that will go on at six to hear what has happened in the world
I wonder what? because in this neighborhood everything has happened.

(Translated by Ellen G. Matilla)

initials

> to put a sign on this closed door
> is to fill it with ribbons and broken designs
> that no one will ever understand.

to try to silence the eyes of death
the troubles that whip and search the eyes, the lips
behind the stairway, in front of the buses
with hands of cold, meager before the evidence of the new
to find yourself isolated before variety, indifferent to the smiles
—the sun is a red button in the sky that turned pale
and suddenly they put it out—
to hoist the flag of sweat before the grace of children
like one who raises the dream from any bed
to find the soft spot of the seats in the afternoon
brought by the collectors, the noise, the hot bath,
the plates of rice and the same pink corner . . .
to try to make the hand cover all the quiet nameless dreams
to return at night to the emptiness made by afternoons of sun
when they penetrate the corners where was left squatting
in wait, a message, a call, a glass of rum, a note on the door

sin timbre, la bicicleta
la tarde sin el tú de un café caliente
comprendo amigo tu hora callada, la víspera de tu sueño roto, lleno de voces que descubren
nuevas voces con promesas y proyecciones de tesoros que sólo son maldiciones
abrir estos ojos mutilados como brazos cortos
dentro de esas tardes sin regreso . . . la caminata es falsa
no hay torniquete para la vida cuando ésta se desparrama
en las cavidades del pecho
nadie conoce los silencios que son sólo ecos de una locura
y frío, mucho frío en la superficie de la cara
por qué no se revienta y se llora?
nadie sabe, es un abecedario único, cerrado por una puerta sin guardianes
y la voz repetía lo que alguien le dijo—
lo dijo la yerba en su alucinación profética una noche en el murmullo del grupo
se cumpliría allá —allá donde la tierra es más caliente—
nadie busca en las libretas de nombre tu apellido
me lo dijo o lo leí en algún sitio
las tardes de domingo son las más propicias, cuando las calamidades
se atraviesan una a una en el centro de la garganta
hasta dejar saber con su mensaje de muerte que los suicidas son sus propios héroes.

without a bell, the bicycle
the afternoon without the you of a hot coffee
I understand my friend your quiet hour, the eve of your broken dream, filled with voices that discover
new voices with promises and projections of treasures that are only curses
to open those mutilated eyes like short arms
in those afternoons without return . . . the long walk is false
there is no tourniquet for life when this overflows
the cavities of the chest
no one knows the silences that are only the echoes of an insanity
and cold, much cold in the surface of the face
why not burst out crying?
no one knows, it is a unique abc, closed by an unguarded door
and the voice repeated what someone told it—
the grass said it in her prophetic hallucination one night in the murmur of the group
would be fulfilled there—there where the earth is hotter—
no one looks for your name in the address book
he told me or I read it somewhere
sunday afternoons are the best, when the troubles
crisscross to the center of the throat
until they let you know with your message of death that suicides are their own heroes

(Translated by Ellen G. Matilla)

Felipe Luciano (b. 1947)

Message to a Dope Fiend . . .

Spics going to the cooker
never realizing they've
been cooked
Mind shook, money took
And nothing to show for it
but raw scars, railroad tracks
on swollen arms
And abscesses of the mind

Go ahead spic
Stick it in your trigger finger
You ain't got nothing to lose
but your freedom
And yo' mama—who wails futilely at
the toilet door
wants to tear down the whole plumbing structure
but can't
'cause you still inside
shooting up, when you already been shot

You ain't got nothing to lose but your freedom
Shoot the poison, the smack of your oppressor
Shoot Papi, on 8th Ave. pulling a mule
  cart
of cheap dresses
to be sold en la Marqueta
Shoot Mami, sweating like her brown ancestors
long ago, killed by Columbus and the Church,
to make that 60.00 in the tombs called factories
Machines rape your mother everyday and
  spit her out
a whore—
Don't throw dagger stares at men
who cruelly crunch your
sisters buttocks between

Mensaje a un tecato

Spics que van al caldero
sin darse cuenta
que se los comieron
Cerebro lavado, dinero robado
Y nada a cambio
excepto cicatrices en carne viva y vías de tren
en unos brazos hinchados
Y abcesos en la mente

Sigue adelante spic
métetela ahí, en el dedo del gatillo
Tú no tienes ná' que perder
excepto tu libertad
Y tu vieja—que se lamenta inutilmente
en la puerta del baño
queriendo derribar toda la plomería
pero no puede
porque tú todavía estás ahí adentro
disparándotela, cuando ya has sido liquidado

Tú no tienes ná' que perder excepto tu libertad
Dispárate ese veneno azote de tu opresor
Dispárate a Papi, el de la octava avenida arrastrando un
carro
de trajes baratos
que serán vendidos en la Marqueta
Dispárate a Mami, sudando como sus antepasados oscuros
asesinados por Colón y la Iglesia hace mucho tiempo,
para ganarse esos 60.00 en tumbas llamadas "factorías"
Máquinas que ultrajan diariamente a tu madre y
la escupen
una puta—
No mires mal a los hombres
que cruelmente agarran
las nalgas de tu hermana entre

slimy fingers
You ain't doing nothing
to change it spic
You ain't got nothing to lose
but your freedom

Shoot up our island
of Borinquen
populated by writhing snakes
who we nicely call gringos
Green Go
Green Go
Green Berets en el Yunque
Green Marines on Calle del Sol
Green bills passing from hand
to calloused palms,
and you shoot the poison 'cause you don't
want to stare at your own ugly reflection—
But it's there spic, hanging off the stoops,
dripping over on firescapes, in the eyes
of your hermanito, who wants to be
like you—when he grows up

Better get hip—Quit lying &
jiving
& flying like you own something
'cause you don't own nothing but your chains
And when the revolution comes
very, very soon—you shoot, and I'll shoot
You shoot & I'll shoot, you shoot & I'll shoot—
And unless you shoot straight,
I'm gonna get you
Before you get yourself!

The Library

Been seduced once or twice
The N.Y. Public Library raped me
viciously

sus dedos limosos
Si tú no haces ná'
pa' cambiarlo spic
Tú no tienes ná' que perder
excepto tu libertad

Dispárate tu isla
de Borinquen
poblada de culebras retorciéndose
a quienes delicadamente llamamos gringos
Green Go
Green Go
Boinas Verdes en el Yunque
Marinos Verdes en la calle Sol
Billetes Verdes pasando de manos
a palmas callosas,
y tú te disparas el veneno porque no quieres
mirar tu propio reflejo—
Pero está ahí spic, vagando por las entradas,
escurriéndose por las escaleras de escape, en los ojos
de tu hermanito, que quiere ser
como tú—cuando sea grande

Ponte en algo—Déjate de embustes y de hablar tanta mierda
y de volar como si algo te perteneciera
porque no te pertenece nada sino tus cadenas
Y cuando llegue la revolución
pronto, muy pronto—tú disparas y yo disparo
Tú disparas y yo disparo, tú disparas y yo disparo—
Y si no disparas bien
yo te voy a coger
Antes de que tú te cojas tú mismo

(Traducción: Ángel Luis Méndez)

La biblioteca

Me han seducido una o dos veces
La Biblioteca Pública de Nueva York me violó viciosamente

Assaulted my nose with book smells
'Til I almost forgot
Revolution was a thing of the streets.
Men with herringbones and blue shirts
and thick-rimmed glasses have signs on them
That point to Flatbush
and the rabbi insisted that scholars and crematoriums
were Compatible.
Young whites, poring over books
Memorizing but never learning
and I wonder how they'll justify genocide.
"I was in the library, honest to God,
  I didn't even know."
Don't matter. The library tempts me
Sometimes worse than a woman
With wide baby-holding hips and thick
  calves
Sometimes I wanna sleep on it, in it, through it
  and
Wake up and say, "Good morning books."
I've kissed books before, held them
  close to my brown skin
Learned why my mother got moody at the end of every
  month
But they never taught me how to fight
Or how to run from cops sperm bullets
"Zig zag, Butchy, zig zag, don't run straight fool."
Taught me to know, but not to believe
Moms believe in God
I believe in revolution
We both believe in something
Devoutly.
So,
I guess I'll always be tempted
And sometimes raped.
"Got to go home now books. It's ten o'clock
and you're closing up.
God, I wish I could fuck you. G'nite."

me asaltó la nariz con un olor a libros
hasta que casi olvidé
que la Revolución es una cosa de la calle.
Hombres con gabanes y camisas azules
con gruesos espejuelos y letreros
que apuntan hacia Flatbush
y un rabino insiste que los eruditos y los crematorios
eran Compatibles.
Jóvenes blancos sumergidos en los libros
memorizando pero nunca aprendiendo
y yo me pregunto cómo justificarán el genocidio.
"Yo estaba en la biblioteca y por Dios Santo que no me
había dado ni cuenta."
No importa. A veces la biblioteca me tienta
mucho más que una mujer
de piernas gruesas y caderas anchas ca-
paces de sostener niños
A veces yo quisiera dormir sobre ella, en ella, a través de
ella
despertar y decir "Libros, buenos días."
Yo he besado libros en otras ocasiones y los he tenido
cerca de mi piel oscura
Y he aprendido el por qué mi madre se malhumoraba al
final de cada mes
Pero ellos nunca me enseñarán cómo pelear
O cómo correrle a la "jara" y a sus balas de esperma
"Zigzag, Butchy, zigzig, no corras derecho pendejo."
Me enseñaron a conocer pero no a creer
La vieja cree en Dios
Yo creo en la revolución
Los dos creemos en algo
Devotamente.
Pues
yo supongo que siempre seré tentado
Y a veces violado.
"Libros, ahora tengo que irme a casa. Son las diez
y ustedes van a cerrar.
Dios, desearía joderte. Buenas noches."

(Traducción: Ángel Luis Méndez)

Víctor Hernández Cruz (b. 1949)

Back to/Back to

o mondays is o.k./last monday a building
  fell
so what
o moving back now   back to
back

i never go back to georgia
i never go back to georgia

packing
man what strange shit you taking
back
man what big shits you pushing

any
how

moving let's go
let's go fast up up up
where
by the candy store   la vieja
la vieja is still alive &
cuchifritos & rice & beans by
la bodega de pepe   by the corner
anti-poverty housing toms
by chelas & the kids yelling & pushing
people down

hey hey
what's happening
qué pasa

Volver a/volver a

vaya los lunes son chéveres/el lunes pasado se cayó un
edificio
y qué
ah volver ahora   volver a
volver

i never go back to georgia
i never go back to georgia

empacando
man que mucha porquería
te llevas
man pero qué mucha mierda estás hablando

como
quiera

mudándonos vámonos
vámonos volando p'arriba arriba arriba
p'adónde
al lado del candy store   *la vieja*
la vieja todavía está viva y
los cuchifritos y el arroz y las habichuelas cerca de
la bodega de pepe   en la esquina
los vividores de la pobreza
cerca de chela y los nenes gritando y tumbando
gente

mira mira
what's happening
qué pasa

o new walls
talking loudly

o monday is o.k.
monday is o.k.

Cocaine Galore 1

eyes that rolled on the floor/as they played
mary/lou did the drinks/the last supper
head of wines/someone stepped on the eyes
of color/colors/on the walls from the eyes.
the building dropped the floor/mary/lou of
funny walks/sister of *leans*/hurry up with
the drinks/shit/as they played/the curtain
began to bleed/& the eyes/the eyes you know/
jingle bells/everyday of new/everyday
  of things/
everyday sunshine/spoons & bags everyday/.

the bad smells of the air/come up coney island/
rackets go round & round/shadows of the sun/
moon & moonglow/the moon is in the water/
line of magic rays/rockets of fourth of july/
independence day/another thing/again/again
colors/colors shooting in the night/red & dark
blue/noise of water/heavy coming/distance
roar of trains/sandals sunk in the sand/half
ass/half/ass wet/half/ass wind/breeze/
  breeze
or what you call it/bad things thruout the night/
up away/your ears with them/

BLAH SHA BLAH BALA
kingsize smoke/out of space/brooklyn bums

ah nuevas paredes
hablando duro

vaya los lunes son chéveres
los lunes son chéveres

(Traducción: Ángel Luis Méndez)

Cocaína en abundancia I

ojos que se arrastran por el piso/mientras ellos tocaban
mary-lou preparó los tragos/la última cena
arrebato de muchos vinos/alguien pisoteó los ojos
del color/colores/sobre la pared desde los ojos
al edificio se le cayó el piso/mary-lou de
caminar cuquero/hermana de recostarse/avanza
con los tragos/carajo/mientras ellos tocaban/la cortina
comenzó a sangrar/y los ojos/tú sabes/los ojos/
jingle bells/todos los días/de nuevo/todos los días/
de cosas/
todos los días/*sunshine*/cucharas y bolsas todos los días/

los malos olores del aire/elévate coney island/
el bullicio da vueltas y vueltas/sombras en el sol/
luna y rayos de luna/la luna está en el agua/
una línea de rayos mágicos/cohetes del cuatro de julio/
día de la independencia/otra pendejá/de nuevo/otra vez
los colores/colores disparándose en la noche/rojo y azul
marino/ruido del agua/una venida del carajo/lejanía
rugidos de tren/sandalias hundidas en la arena/pendejo
y medio/pendejo y medio ensopao/viento pendejo/brisa/
brisa
o como se llame/ruidos fuertes durante toda la noche/
elevándose/yéndose/y tus oídos con ellos/

BLAH SHA BLAH BALA
un gran yerbazo/por fuera/atómicos de brooklyn

pickpocket thru the crowd/big fire of bright
ness brings day/darkness/darkness/& the iron
horse/kicking in loudly/outside/dark/dark
life/
the ladies of the boogaloo going by in hands/or
out of hands/in slow steps going by to cabs or
subways/the corners full with wide/eyed zombies
of the strange parts trying to buy a night for
themselves/mary/lou & plate of mofongo/sunday
morning/sunshine/sitting back eyes closed/

The Fiction Magazine/Volume One

Chapter One

here in the yellow
walls of Grove Street
California
thinking by the poster
of Geronimo his
eagle eyes looking
watching down the
stairs day luz
night too

the five ton truck will
come early in the mor
ning and slip on to
the roads leading to
la playa he said
"you can see cows moos"
bring conga drums
messages down to fish
civilizations to
ride the current

carteristas en el gentío/gran fuego de claridad
trae la mañana/oscuridad/oscuridad/y el caballo
de hierro/pateando ruidosamente/afuera/oscuro/la vida
oscura/
las damas del boogaloo pasan acompañadas/o
solas/con paso lento hacia los taxis o los
subways/las esquinas llenas de zombis de sitios raros
y ojos de par en par tratando de comprarse una
noche/mary-lou y un plato de mofongo/domingo
por la mañana/*sunshine*/recostado con los ojos cerrados/

(Traducción: Ángel Luis Méndez)

La revista de ficción/primer volumen

Capítulo Primero

aquí en las paredes
amarillas de Grove Street
California
pensando junto al cartel
de Gerónimo vigilan
sus ojos de águila
escaleras abajo
día *luz*
y la noche también

el camión de cinco toneladas
vendrá temprano en la mañana
y doblará
por la carretera que conduce a
la playa él dijo
"se puede ver el mugir de las vacas"
trae congas
mensajes hasta las civilizaciones
de peces para
cabalgar sobre la corriente

Chapter Two

a loud North Mexican
voice moved the door
opened   it had been
trained in Oakland
years flying from
Los Angeles / the
Angels of the local
press   "The Suit-Zoot
days" he said the
motor was dancing
the key held tight
Ponce/Rico road the
wheels   the truck
just did the mambo
on the wheel dance
halls

Chapter Three

along the narrow
roads   drops to the
green rocks
these Caribbean hands
encircling the brown
wheel and the truck
climbs all the round
shape of California
the Sun up over the
windows   Geronimo
sticking his head from
one of the rays

Chapter Four

the waves elevate
themselves standing on
the wet sand   at the
edge of the Pacific
the in coming tide
telling tales of Madrid

Capítulo Segundo

una voz fuerte del norte de México
empujó la puerta
abrió había sido
entrenada en Oakland
años volando desde
Los Angeles / los
ángeles de la prensa
local "Los días del traje
Zoot" él dijo el
motor está bailando
la llave fuertemente apretada
Ponce/Rico encaminó las
ruedas el camión
acaba de bailar un mambo
en el dancing hall de
las ruedas

Capítulo Tercero

por las carreteras
estrechas caídas hasta
las rocas verdes
estas manos caribeñas
que abarcan el guía
braun y el camión
sube por toda la forma
redonda de California
el sol sobre
las ventanas Gerónimo
sacando la cabeza
por uno de los rayos

Capítulo Cuarto

las olas se levantan
solas parado en
la arena húmeda al
borde del Pacífico
la marea que sube
contando historias de Madrid

and Aztec book shelfs
and where Cortes took
that Prince   he rolled
down her necklace
and stole both her legs
the ocean declared
till the moon ate the
ceiling.

The Cha Cha Cha at Salt Lake City Bus Terminal

flys ate the apple pie
as I waited for my two eggs
in this gorgeous spaceship waiting
room . . . which is open all night
long . . . the street outside was trampled
by pigeons . . . who seemed to be the only
ones doing the cha cha cha

the juke box was blue
and looked like a computer
sitting under a mid western
landscape painting . . .

I played the Supremes "Baby Love"
a couple of years off . . . but it was
there . . . the closest thing to cha cha
there was nothing more . . . one more
selection . . . the light was still on . . .

I took a chance with the *Salt Lake City*
Country Boys (number M-5) "The House
By The Hill, Is Our Dream House Baby"

y estanterías aztecas
y donde Cortés cojió de pendejo
a aquel príncipe
y se le bajó a ella desde el cuello
y le robó las dos piernas
lo declaró el mar
hasta que la luna se comió
el techo.

(Traducción: Ángel Luis Méndez)

El cha-cha-chá en el terminal de guaguas de Salt Lake City

mientras esperaba el desayuno
en esta lujosa sala espaciada . . .
que nunca cierra . . . las
moscas se comían el *pie* de manzana . . .
afuera la calle estaba siendo atropellada por
palomas . . . que parecían ser las
únicas bailando el cha-cha-chá

la vellonera estaba triste
y bajo uno de esos cuadros que tienen
paisajes del medio oeste
parecía una computadora

yo eché "Baby Love" de las Supremes
pasada dos años . . . pero allí
estaba . . . lo más parecido a un cha-cha-chá
no había nada más . . . un disco
más . . . la lucecita todavía estaba prendida . . .

me arriesgué y escogí el *Salt Lake City
Country Boys* (número M-5) "La casita
en la lomita es nuestro anhelo, amor"

(Traducción: Ángel Luis Méndez)

Etnairis Rivera (b. 1949)

Carta a Manuel

Lista
lista estoy
para decir
esas cosas
que conoces
                    y las temes
pero te siguen gustando
como gustaban ayer
a los tres años
peleándonos por la bola
y la atención de la familia
bola-familia rodando sobre nosotros
la bola la ganabas tú
la atención nos la llevaba la vecina
con la tunda de su marido,
se enredaba entre las patas de la abuela
se encajonaba en el televisor
saltaba años
                    hasta gente que no conocíamos
pero que odiábamos tanto
¿recuerdas?
por ladrones
robándonos palmaditas de los tíos
tus padres que eran los míos
mis padres que eran los tuyos
entonces . . .

Luego
decidimos
hacernos indios
y mezclar las sangres
y era la misma sangre

Letter to Manuel

Ready
I'm ready
to say
those things
that you know
                    and fear
but you keep liking them
the way you liked them yesterday
at the age of three
fighting for the ball
and the family's attention
ball-family rolling over us
the ball you won
the neighbor got the attention
through the beatings from her husband,
it became entangled between the grandmother's legs
was boxed in the television
jumped years
                    even people that we didn't know
but we hated so much
remember?
for robbing us
stealing praise from the uncles
your parents that were mine
my parents that were yours
then . . .

Eventually
we decided
to become Indians
and mix our blood
the blood wasn't different

y jugábamos un juego
de últimos apellidos
que ya no sería juego
cuando nos enteráramos
"Ahora yo ser hermano
para toda la vida
en todas las batallas
frente a todo enemigo"
y yo repetía lo mismo
copiando tu imagen
de gran cacique altivo
alzando la mano a tu guisa
y estampa.

Pero invadieron las madres
el territorio amigo
y nos empaquetaron a la escuela
tú fuiste a la pública y tu bulto
era azul de cuadritos
azules como mi rabia
de vestir uniforme
distinto al tuyo.

A mí
me enviaron al párvulo
de aquellas monjas ahogadas de calor
con tanto trapo en Puerto Rico
a aprender de carretilla
el "Padre Nuestro
que estás en los cielos"
en lugar de padre nuestro
que estás en la cama
"Venga a nos tu reino"
viniéndose en tu madre
y en la mía.

Y yo creía que nos harían distintos
y yo quería permanecer los mismos
mientras tú bailabas
aquel trompo rojo de cabulla larga

and we played a game
of last names
that would no longer be a game
once we found out
"Now I be your brother
for all our lives
in all battles
before all enemies"
and I repeated the same
imitating your image
of the great high chief
raising my hand in your way
and style.

But the mothers invaded
the friendly territory
and packed us off to school
you went to a public one and your
briefcase was blue plaid
blue as my anger
for wearing uniforms
different from yours.

Me
they sent to the kindergarten
of those nuns drowned in the heat of Puerto Rico
with so many rags
to learn by rote
the "Our Father
Who art in heaven"
instead of our father
who art in bed
"Thy kingdom come"
coming inside your mother
and in mine.

And I thought they would make us different
and I wanted to remain the same
while you spun
that red top with a long cord

en tu recreo,
y descubrías palabras
que sonrojaban a los grandes,
a mí me vestían de ángel
llegado diciembre
peluche por todos lados
molestando mi nariz
o de pastora canasta en mano
a cantar villancicos
que no te entusiasmaban mucho.

Pero supiste mi enojo
más que coraje, pena
de creerte olvidadizo
y me permitiste callejear contigo
por zaguanes misteriosos
empujar ruedas de lata enmohecida
barandilla abajo,
corretear por el castillo
nuestra cueva secreta de piratas.
Así creamos el segundo pacto
"No importa la escuela a que nos manden . . ."
Terminado el amén impaciente
volaba a deshacerme de aquella insignia
padre, chulo y espíritu santo
y me devolvía
a ti
a mi verdad
a deslizarnos con cartones
pescar gupis
jugar al esconder en el cementerio,
pitar a las gringas
de pantalones cortos
y nalgas chumbas
en el Boulevard del Valle.
Esos titeritos de La Perla
necesitando una buena escarmentada
según la gente,
necesitando calor, comida
según nosotros.

during your recess,
and discovered words
that made the big people blush,
me they dressed like an angel
come December
plush on all sides
bothering my nose
or as a shepherdess basket in hand
to sing Christmas carols
that didn't excite you much.

But you knew my displeasure
more than anger, sorrow
of thinking you forgetful
and you let me hang around with you
through mysterious alleys
pushing rusted tin wheels
down the *barandilla*,
run through the castle
our secret pirate cave.
In that way we made our second pact
"It doesn't matter what school they send us to . . ."
Finished with the impatient amen
flew to rid myself of that insignia
father, pimp and holy spirit
and returned
to you
to my truth
to slide with pasteboards
catch guppies
play hide and seek in the cemetery,
whistle at the gringas
with short pants
and flat buttocks
on the Boulevard del Valle.
Those little punks from La Perla
need a good lesson
said the people,
need warmth, need food
we said.

Te llevabas a la gente
aquel día por la calle
en tu prisa de mostrarme
el diploma de Intermedia
que te hacía más grande
más hombre
aquellas letras negras de curvitas
con tu nombre amplio
sin el mío
en aquel papel blanco
pálido como mi cuerpo asmático
desde hacía semanas.
Y te empeñaste en fotografiarnos
con mi pijama y tu diploma
para siempre
el tercer pacto
"No importa las enfermedades . . ."

Tiempo después
tus padres mis tíos
se habían divorciado
de tanto pelear, celar
pelear y abusar
pelear;
tiempo después
mis padres tus tíos
decidieron salir de "allá abajo"
mudarse a Río Piedras
y cargaron conmigo
que lloré todo el viaje,
allá no hay adoquines
allá no hay castillos
pero ellos no entendían
me arrancaron de la ganga
de las calles conocidas
con los ojos cerrados,
me arrancaron de mi barrio
pero no de ti.

En todos los meses

You bumped the people
on the street that day
in your hurry to show me
your Junior High School diploma
that made you bigger
more manly
those black curved letters
with your name enlarged
without mine
on that white paper
pale as my asthmatic body
for several weeks.
And you insisted on photographing us
with my pajamas and your diploma
forever
the third pact
"No matter what illnesses . . ."

Some time later
your parents my uncles
had gotten a divorce
from so much fighting, jealousy
fighting and abuse
fighting;
some time later
my parents your uncles
decided to get out from "down there"
move to Río Piedras
and took me
crying all the way,
over there there are no paving stones
over there there are no castles
but they didn't understand
they pulled me from the gang
off the streets known
with eyes closed,
they pulled me from my neighborhood
but not from you.

In all the months

doce más doce
que pasaban
mientras yo asistía al colegio
de monjas enfermas
desviadas sexuales,
autoritarias empedernidas
tú matabas el tiempo
por no matar a los grandes,
jugando canicas
vendiendo botellas
lo que se te ocurriera
menos ir a la escuela,
porque supiste que pensarían
en tu remedio de mano dura.
Y te plantaron a mi colegio
menos infierno ahora
y volvimos a hablar malo
en la hora de recreo
a robar vellones a los chicos
a halar las trenzas de las pibes.

Pero miraste a Carmen
ojitos de mosca boba
con su pelo moderno
corto y rizado distinto al mío;
le compraste piragua
enviaste una tarjeta ridícula
de corazones
escribiste su nombre
en todas tus libretas.
Yo te escupí los pies
te deseé la muerte
dije mentiras sobre ti
a los maestros
me arrepentí mil veces que hubieras venido.

Estrujé el silencio
por más de una semana
larga como la partida
hasta que dijiste en clase

twelve plus twelve
that passed
while I attended the school
of sick nuns
sexual deviates,
hardened authoritarians
you killed the time,
so as not to kill the older ones,
playing marbles
selling bottles
whatever occurred to you
except going to school,
because you knew what they would think
of your hard-handed methods.
And they put you in my school
less of a hell now
and we returned to talking dirty
during recess
stealing nickels from the kids
and pulling the little girls braids.

But you looked at Carmen
dumb-looking eyes
with her modern hairdo
short and curled different from mine;
you bought her *piraguas*
you sent a ridiculous card
of hearts
wrote her name
in all your notebooks.
I spat at your feet
wished you death
told lies about you
to the teachers
a thousand times regretted you had come.

I crumpled the silence
for over a week
as long as the parting
until you said in class

"Eso lo escribió el Ñoco de Lepanto"
y todos rieron
la maestra rabiaba
le brincaba el pecho
enorme mantecoso
todos se reían
ella más furiosa
y yo supe que eras el mismo
de la mezcla india de sangres
de la cueva de piratas
mi jefe de pandilla
mi sabio títere
mi amor . . .

Ya te habías ido a otro pueblo
sobrepoblado
de largas procesiones
mercados abiertos
y nuevos amigos,
distintos
que hablaban de abusos
de rabia
de tierra nuestra
y enemigo nuestro.
Entendiste por qué
se quemaban banderas
por todo el país
y en el pueblo tuyo
donde tuviste muchas novias,
aprendiste a fumar yerba
y viviste con tu abuela beata
que no se pinta
reza a todas horas
habla a todas horas
pero la quieres,
porque estuviste solo
cuando tus padres se fueron
cada uno por su lado
como hace todo el mundo
y ella te alimentó.

"That was written by the Maimed of Lepanto"
and everybody laughed
the teacher boiled
her chest jumped
enormous greasy
everybody was laughing
she more furious
and I knew you were the same
of the mixing of Indian blood
of the pirate cave
my gang chief
my wise punk
my love . . .

You had already left for another town
overpopulated
                    with long processions
open markets
and new friends,
different
that spoke of abuses
of anger
of our land
of our enemy.
You understood why
                              flags were burned
all over the country
and in your town
where you had many sweethearts,
were turned on to grass
and lived with your blessed grandmother
who doesn't wear make-up
prays all hours
talks all hours
but you love her,
because you were alone
when your parents left
each his own way
as everyone does
and she fed you.

Lista
lista estoy
para decirte
estas cosas
que conoces
y las temes
porque te parecen raras
porque nos creerán monstruos
y nada más hemos vivido
como al Principio
especie con especie
para no sentirnos solos
para sabernos presentes
reconociendo tu voz
y tú la mía
en el silencio
de tantos lapsos que ya te cuento;
amando la misma lucha
conociendo entonces al mismo enemigo
odiando ahora al mismo padre,
Manuel
Lin de los tres años
Manolito de los cinco
Nolo de mi adolescencia
deseando tu espalda
tocarte entre las piernas
como luego lo hice
y te gustó
y me gustó
hasta perder el aire
y repetirlo
Manuel
sin saber que tú
amor
eras mi hermano . . .

Ready
I'm ready
to tell you
those things
that you know
and fear
because they seem strange
because they must think us monsters
and nothing more have we lived
as in the Beginning
species with species
so as not to feel alone
to know us present
recognizing your voice
and you mine
in the silence
of so many lapses that I'll tell you;
loving the same struggle
knowing then the same enemy
hating now the same father,
Manuel
Lin at three
Manolito at five
Nolo of my adolescence
desiring your back
touching you between the legs
as I eventually did
and you liked it
and I liked it
until losing breath
and repeating it
Manuel
without knowing that you
love
are my brother . . .

(Translated by Digna Sánchez-Méndez)

Bibliographies

Luis Llorens Torres (1876–1944)

Al pie de la Alhambra, Granada, Imprenta Viuda e hijos de Sanatel, 1899.
Sonetos sinfónicos, San Juan, Antillana, 1914.
La canción de las Antillas y otros poemas, San Juan, Negociado de Materiales, Imprenta y Transporte, 1929.
Voces de la campana mayor, San Juan, Editorial Puertorriqueña, 1935.
Alturas de América, San Juan, Imprenta Baldrich, 1940.
Poesías, San Juan, Instituto de Cultura Puertorriqueña, 1959.
Obras completas, Vol. I (Poesía), San Juan, Instituto de Cultura Puertorriqueña, 1967.

Evaristo Ribera Chevremont (b. 1896)

Desfile romántico, San Juan, Real Hermanos, n.d. (1914, cf. Margot Arce de Vázquez, Laura Gallego, Luis de Arrigoitia, *Lecturas puertorriqueñas: poesía*, Conn., Troutman Press.)
El templo de los alabastros, Madrid, Ambos Mundos, n.d. (1919, cf. M. Arce *et al.*, *op. cit.*).
La copa de Hebe, Madrid, 1922.
Los almendros del Paseo de Covadonga, San Juan, Puerto Rico Ilustrado, 1928.
Pajarera, San Juan, Poliedro, 1929.
La hora del orífice, San Juan, 1929.

Tierra y sombra, San Juan, El Florete, 1930.
Color, San Juan, Romero, 1938.
Tonos y formas, San Juan, Biblioteca de Autores Puertorriqueños, 1943.
Anclas de oro, San Juan, Imprenta Venezuela, 1945.
Barro, San Juan, Imprenta Venezuela, 1945.
Tú, mar, y yo y ella, Río Piedras, P. R., Junta Editora de la Universidad de Puerto Rico, 1946.
Verbo, San Juan, Imprenta Venezuela, 1947.
Creación, San Juan, Imprenta Venezuela, 1951.
Antología poética (1924–1950) y La llama pensativa (sonetos inéditos) 1950, Madrid, Cultura Hispánica, 1954.
La llama pensativa, San Juan, Imprenta Venezuela, 1955.
Antología poética (1924–1950), Río Piedras, P. R., Universidad de Puerto Rico, 1957.
Cuadernos de poesía, VI, Instituto de Cultura Puertorriqueña, 1960.
Inefable orilla, San Juan, Imprenta Venezuela, 1961.
Punto final, San Juan, Imprenta Venezuela, 1963.
El semblante, Río Piedras, P. R., Universidad de Puerto Rico, 1964.
Principio del canto, San Juan, Imprenta Venezuela, 1965.
Antología poética (1929–1965), San Juan, Editorial del Departamento de Instrucción Pública, 1967.

Juan Antonio Corretjer (b. 1908)

Agüeibana, Ponce, P. R., Tipografía del Llano, 1932.
Ulises, Ponce, Puerto Rico evangélico, 1933.
Amor de Puerto Rico, San Juan, Edición La Palabra, 1937.
El leñero (Poema de la revolución de Lares), New York, 1944.
Los primeros años, San Juan, Casa Baldrich, 1951.
Alabanza en la torre de Ciales, San José, Costa Rica, Repertorio Americano, 1953.
Don Diego en el cariño, San Juan, Editorial La Escrita, 1956.
Distancias, Guaynabo, P. R., Edicones Vel, 1957.
Yerba Bruja, San Juan, Imprenta Venezuela, 1957.
Genio y figura (Rapsodia criolla), Guaynabo, P. R., Litografía Guilliani, 1961.
Pausa para el amor, San Juan, Cooperativa de Artes Gráficas Romualdo Real, 1967.
Canciones de Consuelo, que son canciones de protesta, mimeógrafo, Guaynabo, P. R., Publicaciones de la Liga Socialista Puertorriqueña, 1971.

Francisco Matos Paoli (b. 1915)

Signario de lágrimas, Aguadilla, P. R., Tribuna Libre, 1931.
Cardo labriego y otros poemas, San Juan, Venezuela, 1937.
Habitante del eco (1937–1941), San Juan, Soltero, 1944.
Teoría del olvido, Río Piedras, Junta Editora de la Universidad de Puerto Rico, 1944.
Canto a Puerto Rico, San Juan, Ateneo Puertorriqueño, 1952. First prize: Ateneo Puertorriqueño (1950).
Luz de los héroes, San Juan, Casa Baldrich, 1954.
Criatura del rocío, San Juan, Ateneo Puertorriqueño, 1958.
Canto de la locura, San Juan, Ediciones Juan Ponce de León, 1962.
El viento y la paloma (1961–1963), San Juan, Ediciones Juan Ponce de León, 1969.
Cuadernos de poesía, ed. by José R. de la Torre, San Juan, Instituto de Cultura Puertorriqueña, 1971–.
Cancionero, San Juan, Ediciones Juan Ponce de León, 1971.
La marea sube, San Juan, Ediciones Juan Ponce de León, 1971.
Ser en el alba, San Juan, Ed. Librería Internacional, 1971.
Antología poética, ed. by José E. González, Río Piedras, Editorial Universitaria, 1972.

Luis Palés Matos (1898–1959)

Azaleas, Guayama, P. R., Rodríguez y Cía., 1915.
Tuntún de pasa y grifería, San Juan, Biblioteca de Autores Puertorriqueños, 1937; new edition, 1950; third edition, 1960.
Poesía (1915–1956), Río Piedras, Universidad de Puerto Rico, 1957; fourth revised edition, 1971.
Obra completa, ed. by Margot Arce-Vásquez, Río Piedras, Editorial Universitaria, 1971–.

Julia de Burgos (1914–1953)

Poema en veinte surcos, San Juan, Imprenta Venezuela, 1938.
Canción de la verdad sencilla, San Juan, Imprenta Baldrich, 1939.
El mar y tú, otros poemas, San Juan, Puerto Rico Printing and Publishing Co., 1954.
Obra poética, San Juan, Instituto de Cultura Puertorriqueña, 1961.

Hugo Margenat (1933–1957)

Published in *Orfeo; Guajana* dedicated an issue to him: I, 4, 1963, and posthumously published his poetry.
Lámpara apagada, San Juan, 1954.
Interperie, San Juan, Imprenta Baldrich, 1955.
Mundo abierto, San Juan, Imprenta Baldrich, 1958.
Ventana hacia lo último, San Juan, Imprenta Venezuela, 1960.

José María Lima (b. 1934)

He has published in *Versiones*. Included in *Poesía nueva puertorriqueña*, ed. by Luis A. Rosario Quiles, San Juan, Edil, Producciones Bondo, 1971.
Homenaje al ombligo (with Ángela Maria Dávila), Puerto Rico, n.d. (1967).

Iris M. Zavala (b. 1936)

Has published in *Asomante, Revista del Instituto de Cultura Puertorriqueña, Pájaro Cascabel* (Mexico), *Sur* (Argentina).
Barro doliente, Santander, Publicaciones La Isla de los Ratones, 1964. First Prize in Puerto Rican Literature (1964).
Poemas prescindibles, N. Y.–Buenos Aires, La Librería, 1971.

Luis A. Rosario Quiles (b. 1936)

Has published in *Poesía Española* (Madrid), *Mester, Versiones*. Was director of *Versiones*.
La vida que pedí, San Juan, 1958.
El juicio de Víctor Campolo, San Juan, Ediciones Bondo, 1970.

Alfredo Matilla (b. 1937)

He has published in *Versiones, Amaru* (Perú), *Guajana*.

Marina Arzola (b. 1939)

Has published in *Alma Latina, Bayoán, Prometeo, Palestra, Guajana, Asomante, Revista del Instituto de Cultura Puertorriqueña, La Nueva Sangre* (N.Y.), *Surcos*. Included in: *Cantos a Puerto Rico*, Instituto de Cultura Puertorriqueña, 1968, and in *Poesía nueva puertorriqueña*, ed. by Luis A. Rosario Quiles, San Juan, Edil, Producciones Bondo, 1971. First Prize of the Ateneo Puertorriqueño with "El niño de cristal y los olvidados" (1966).
Palabras vivas, Barcelona, Editorial Rumbos, 1968.

Juan Sáez Burgos (b. 1943)

He has published in *Guajana, Bayoán, Asomante, Versiones, Prometeo;* he is included in *Antología de jóvenes poetas,* Instituto de Cultura Puertorriqueña, 1965, and in *Poesía nueva puertorriqueña,* ed. by Luis A. Rosario Quiles, Edil, Producciones Bondo, 1971; First Prize: Ateneo Puertorriqueño (1963), with *Un hombre para el llanto.* Honorable Mention-Ateneo Puertorriqueño (1970).

Un hombre para el llanto, Río Piedras, Edil, 1969.

Pedro Pietri (b. 1944)

He has published in *P'alante* (N.Y.), *Unidad Latina* (N. Y.), and in *Revista del Instituto de Estudios Puertorriqueños* (Brooklyn College, N. Y.).

Pedro Pietri en Casa Puerto Rico (Long-playing record)

A Serious Monster Picture, Central Park Publications (N.Y.), 1971 (film).

Jorge María Ruscalleda Bercedóniz (b. 1944)

Has published in *Instante, Mester, Versiones, Guajana.* Included in *Poesía nueva puertorriqueña,* ed. by Luis A. Rosario Quiles, 1971. Editor of *Mester.*

Posesión de plena permanencia, Aguadilla, P. R., Los Quijotes, 1966.

Ángela María Dávila (b. 1944)

Has published in *Versiones, Guajana, Prometeo.* Included in *Poesía nueva puertorriqueña,* ed. by Luis A. Rosario Quiles, 1971.

Homenaje al ombligo (with José María Lima), Puerto Rico, n.d. (1967).

Billy Cajigas (b. 1944)

Has published in *Mester* and *Revista del Instituto de Estudios Puertorriqueños* (Brooklyn College, N. Y.). Included in *Headway,* ed. by L. Michael, New York, Holt, Rinehart and Winston, 1970, and in *Poesía nueva puertorriqueña,* ed. by Luis A. Rosario Quiles, San Juan, Edil, Producciones Bondo, 1971.

Iván Silén (b. 1944)

He has published in *Mester, Versiones, La Nueva Sangre* (N. Y.), *Norte* (Holland), *El Rehilete* (Mexico), *Revista del Instituto de Estudios Puertorriqueños* (Brooklyn College, N. Y.). Included in *Poesía nueva puertorriqueña,* ed. by Luis A. Rosario Quiles, San Juan, Edil, Producciones Bondo, 1971.

Después del suicidio, Santo Domingo (Dominican Republic), El Caribe, 1970.

El pájaro-loco, San Juan, Internacional, n.d. (1972).

Edwin Reyes Berríos (b. 1944)

He has published in *Guajana, Bayoán, Prometeo, Palestra, Claridad.*

Ángel Luis Méndez (b. 1944)

He has published in the *Revista del Instituto de Estudios Puertorriqueños* (Brooklyn College, N. Y.).

Felipe Luciano (b. 1947)

Has published in *YLO* (New York), *P'alante* (New York) *Right on!* (film)

Víctor Hernández Cruz (b. 1949)

Has published in *Evergreen Review, New York Review of Books, Ramparts, Down Here, Umbra, Revista del Instituto de Estudios Puertorriqueños* (Brooklyn College, N.Y.). Was editor of *Umbra.* Included in *An Anthology of Afro-American Writing,* ed. by LeRoi Jones and Larry Neal, W. Morrow & Co., Inc., 1968.

Papo Got His Gun, New York, Calle Once Publications, 1966.

Snaps, New York, Random House, 1969.

Etnairis Rivera (b. 1949)

Has published in *Mester, Guajana, Versiones, Palestra, Revista del Instituto de Estudios Puertorriqueños* (Brooklyn College, N.Y.), *La Nueva Sangre* (N.Y.). Included in *Poesía nueva puertorriqueña,* ed. by Luis A. Rosario Quiles, San Juan, Edil, Producciones Bondo, 1971.